Dinosaur Fact Book

For Adults

Crafted by Skriuwer

Table of Contents

Introduction

Welcome to the World of Dinosaurs

Dinosaurs have captured our imagination for generations. From the towering giants that once ruled the Earth to the smaller, feathered creatures that hinted at the future of avian life, these ancient beings continue to fascinate and inspire. But beyond the Hollywood blockbusters and children's toys lies a rich, complex history that spans over 165 million years—a history filled with incredible facts that tell the story of a world long gone.

In this book, **"Dinosaur Fact Book for Adults,"** we're diving deep into the world of dinosaurs, uncovering 1,000 fascinating facts that reveal the true nature of these prehistoric giants. Whether you're a seasoned dinosaur enthusiast or just curious about these magnificent creatures, this book will offer something new and engaging at every turn.

What to Expect

This isn't just another dinosaur book filled with dry statistics and scientific jargon. Instead, we've structured this book to be a conversation—an exploration of the world of dinosaurs that feels as exciting as discovering a new fossil yourself. We'll cover everything from the Triassic beginnings to the catastrophic events that wiped them out, and we'll explore the latest in paleontological research to keep you updated on what modern science is uncovering about these ancient beings.

Each chapter is dedicated to a different aspect of dinosaur life, from their evolution and types to their behaviors and eventual extinction. You'll find sections that break down complex concepts into easy-to-understand facts, while still maintaining the depth and detail that make these creatures so fascinating. Whether you're interested in the colossal Sauropods or the ferocious Theropods, or perhaps you want to delve into the social structures and daily lives of these creatures, there's something here for you.

Why Dinosaurs Matter

So why do we continue to be fascinated by dinosaurs? Perhaps it's because they represent a world so different from our own—an era where creatures we can hardly imagine walked the Earth. Dinosaurs also remind us of the fragility of life, of how even the mightiest creatures can be wiped out by the forces of nature. They provide us with a sense of awe, a reminder of the natural world's power and mystery.

But beyond the wonder, studying dinosaurs also offers valuable insights into biology, evolution, and Earth's history. Understanding how these creatures lived, adapted, and eventually perished gives us clues about our own world and our place within it.

How to Use This Book

This book is organized into chapters that each cover a specific topic about dinosaurs. Whether you read it from cover to cover or jump to the sections that most intrigue you, you'll find that each chapter is filled with carefully curated facts designed to spark your curiosity and expand your knowledge. Alongside the facts, you'll also find illustrations that bring these creatures to life, helping you visualize the scale, diversity, and uniqueness of the dinosaur world.

A Journey into the Past

As you turn the pages, you'll be embarking on a journey through time, back to an era when giants roamed the Earth. You'll learn about the incredible diversity of dinosaurs, the environments they lived in, and the challenges they faced. From the awe-inspiring to the downright bizarre, this book will showcase the many wonders of the dinosaur age.

So, let's step into the time machine and travel back millions of years. Let's explore the Mesozoic era and meet the dinosaurs—creatures that, though long extinct, continue to live on in our imaginations and in the pages of history.

Chapter 1: The Age of Dinosaurs

Life Before the Dinosaurs and the Mesozoic Era

When we think of dinosaurs, we often picture them as the dominant life forms on Earth. However, their reign was just one chapter in the planet's long history. Before dinosaurs ever set foot on the Earth, other creatures roamed, and the planet itself underwent dramatic changes. Understanding this prelude gives us a richer context for the age of dinosaurs—a period that spanned over 165 million years and is collectively known as the Mesozoic Era.

Fact 1: The Earth is Over 4.5 Billion Years Old

Long before dinosaurs, the Earth formed around 4.54 billion years ago from a swirling cloud of gas and dust left over from the Sun's formation. The planet's early years were turbulent, with frequent volcanic activity, meteorite impacts, and a surface that was more molten than solid. It wasn't until the crust cooled and solidified that conditions became favorable for life to emerge.

Fact 2: Life Began in the Oceans

The first forms of life on Earth appeared in the oceans about 3.5 billion years ago, in the form of simple, single-celled organisms. These tiny creatures dominated the planet for billions of years, with complex life forms evolving much later. The Cambrian Explosion, around 541 million years ago, marked a significant increase in the diversity of life, leading to the development of most major animal groups, including some of the ancestors of dinosaurs.

Fact 3: The Pre-Dinosaur World Was Ruled by Amphibians and Reptiles

Before dinosaurs emerged, the world was dominated by amphibians and early reptiles. During the Carboniferous period, around 359 to 299 million years ago, vast swampy forests covered much of the Earth, and amphibians were among the largest land animals. As the climate changed and became drier, reptiles began to thrive, leading to the rise of the ancestors of dinosaurs.

Fact 4: The Permian Mass Extinction Set the Stage for Dinosaurs

About 252 million years ago, the Earth experienced the most devastating mass extinction event in its history, known as the Permian-Triassic extinction event. This "Great Dying" wiped out about 90% of marine species and 70% of terrestrial vertebrates. The cause is still debated, with theories ranging from massive volcanic eruptions to asteroid impacts and methane release from the ocean floor. Whatever the cause, this event drastically altered Earth's ecosystems, allowing dinosaurs to rise in the aftermath.

Fact 5: The Mesozoic Era is Divided into Three Periods

The Mesozoic Era, often called the "Age of Dinosaurs," is divided into three major periods: the Triassic, Jurassic, and Cretaceous. Each period had its own unique climate, geography, and dominant species.

- **Triassic Period (252 to 201 million years ago):** This period began in the wake of the Permian extinction. The early part of the Triassic saw the emergence of the first true dinosaurs. The supercontinent Pangaea still existed, and the climate was generally hot and dry.

- **Jurassic Period (201 to 145 million years ago):** During the Jurassic, Pangaea began to break apart into smaller continents. The climate became more humid, leading to lush forests that supported the growth of large herbivorous dinosaurs like the Brachiosaurus. The Jurassic is also when many of the most famous dinosaurs, like the Stegosaurus and Allosaurus, lived.

- **Cretaceous Period (145 to 66 million years ago):** The final period of the Mesozoic Era saw the further breakup of continents and the rise of flowering plants. The Cretaceous is perhaps the most famous period for dinosaurs, as it featured giants like the Tyrannosaurus rex and the Triceratops. This period ended with another mass extinction, wiping out the dinosaurs and paving the way for mammals to rise.

Fact 6: The Mesozoic Climate Was Generally Warm

One of the defining features of the Mesozoic Era was its warm climate. For much of this era, the Earth was warmer than it is today, with no polar ice caps. This warm climate allowed for the flourishing of lush vegetation, which in turn supported the massive herbivorous dinosaurs. The lack of significant ice at the poles also meant higher sea levels and the formation of shallow inland seas that covered large parts of the continents.

Fact 7: The World Was Once a Single Supercontinent

At the beginning of the Mesozoic Era, all of Earth's landmasses were joined together in a single supercontinent called Pangaea. This massive landmass stretched from pole to pole and was surrounded by a vast ocean known as Panthalassa. As the Mesozoic progressed, Pangaea slowly began to break apart due to the movement of tectonic plates. This breakup had significant impacts on the climate, ocean circulation, and the evolution of life, including the dinosaurs.

Fact 8: The First Dinosaurs Appeared in the Late Triassic

Dinosaurs first appeared around 230 million years ago, during the late Triassic period. These early dinosaurs were relatively small and bipedal, with most species being no larger than a modern-day dog. One of the earliest known dinosaurs is Eoraptor, a small, carnivorous dinosaur that lived in what is now Argentina. These early dinosaurs quickly diversified, leading to the wide variety of species that would dominate the Jurassic and Cretaceous periods.

Fact 9: Dinosaurs Were Part of a Larger Group Called Archosaurs

Dinosaurs are part of a larger group of reptiles known as archosaurs, which also includes modern crocodiles and birds, as well as the extinct pterosaurs. Archosaurs were characterized by specific features in their skulls, including openings in front of the eyes and on the lower jaw, which helped to lighten the skull and provide space for muscles. This group first appeared in the Triassic period, and dinosaurs quickly became the most successful branch of this group.

Fact 10: Not All Reptiles of the Mesozoic Were Dinosaurs

While dinosaurs were the dominant land animals of the Mesozoic, not all reptiles from this era were dinosaurs. The seas were home to a variety of marine reptiles, such as the long-necked plesiosaurs and the dolphin-like ichthyosaurs. In the skies, pterosaurs ruled as the first vertebrates capable of powered flight. These creatures, while contemporaries of the dinosaurs, belonged to different branches of the reptile family tree.

Fact 11: The Triassic-Jurassic Extinction Helped Dinosaurs Thrive

Another significant extinction event occurred at the end of the Triassic period, about 201 million years ago. This event wiped out many of the large amphibians and reptiles that had dominated earlier in the Mesozoic, creating ecological niches that dinosaurs quickly filled. This extinction event helped set the stage for the dinosaurs to become the dominant land animals during the Jurassic and Cretaceous periods.

Fact 12: The Jurassic Was a Time of Giant Herbivores

The Jurassic period is perhaps most famous for its giant herbivorous dinosaurs, such as the long-necked sauropods. These massive creatures, including Brachiosaurus and Diplodocus, could grow to lengths of over 80 feet and weigh as much as 80 tons. The lush, tropical forests and abundant plant life of the Jurassic provided ample food for these giants, allowing them to grow to such enormous sizes.

Fact 13: The First Birds Appeared in the Late Jurassic

One of the most significant evolutionary developments of the Jurassic period was the appearance of the first birds. Archaeopteryx, discovered in the late Jurassic, is often considered the first bird. This creature had feathers and wings but also retained many dinosaur-like features, such as teeth and a long bony tail. The evolution of birds from theropod dinosaurs is one of the most well-documented examples of evolutionary transition.

Fact 14: The Cretaceous Period Saw the Rise of Flowering Plants

While the Jurassic period was dominated by conifers, ferns, and other non-flowering plants, the Cretaceous period saw the rise of angiosperms, or flowering plants. This development had a profound impact on the ecosystems of the time, as flowering plants provided new sources of food for herbivorous dinosaurs and helped shape the evolution of plant-eating species. The spread of flowering plants also contributed to the diversification of insect species, which in turn affected the entire food chain.

Fact 15: The Cretaceous-Paleogene Extinction Ended the Age of Dinosaurs

The Mesozoic Era came to a dramatic end about 66 million years ago with the Cretaceous-Paleogene (K-Pg) extinction event. This mass extinction wiped out nearly 75% of Earth's species, including all non-avian dinosaurs. The most widely accepted theory is that a massive asteroid impact, combined with volcanic activity and climate change, caused this extinction. The evidence for this includes a layer of iridium-rich clay found around the world, which is associated with asteroid impacts, and the Chicxulub crater in the Yucatan Peninsula, which is believed to be the impact site.

Fact 16: Birds are the Last Surviving Dinosaurs

Though most dinosaurs perished in the K-Pg extinction, their legacy lives on in the form of birds. Modern birds are the direct descendants of small, feathered theropods, making them the last surviving lineage of dinosaurs. This evolutionary connection has been supported by numerous fossil discoveries and studies of bird anatomy, genetics, and behavior.

Fact 17: Dinosaurs Shaped the Evolution of Modern Animals

The dominance of dinosaurs during the Mesozoic had a significant impact on the evolution of other species. For example, mammals first appeared in the late Triassic but remained small and relatively inconspicuous during the age of dinosaurs. It was only after the extinction of dinosaurs that mammals were able to diversify and occupy many of the ecological niches left vacant by the dinosaurs. The adaptations that allowed dinosaurs to thrive, such as bipedalism and warm-bloodedness, also influenced the evolution of later species.

Fact 18: Dinosaur Fossils are Found on Every Continent

Dinosaur fossils have been discovered on every continent, including Antarctica. This global distribution is a testament to the success and adaptability of dinosaurs during the Mesozoic. The presence of fossils in Antarctica suggests that, at the time, the continent was much warmer and supported a diverse range of life. The discovery of fossils in different parts of the world has provided invaluable insights into the diversity of dinosaur species and the environments they lived in.

Fact 19: Paleontologists Use Technology to Study Dinosaurs

Modern paleontology relies heavily on technology to study dinosaur fossils. Techniques such as CT scanning, 3D modeling, and isotopic analysis allow scientists to examine fossils in unprecedented detail. For example, CT scans can reveal the internal structure of bones without damaging them, providing insights into how dinosaurs moved, breathed, and grew. Isotopic analysis can shed light on the diets and migration patterns of dinosaurs by examining the chemical composition of their bones and teeth.

Fact 20: The Study of Dinosaurs is Constantly Evolving

Our understanding of dinosaurs has evolved dramatically over the past few decades, thanks to new discoveries and advances in technology. The image of dinosaurs as slow, lumbering reptiles has been replaced by a more dynamic picture of active, warm-blooded animals. New fossil finds continue to challenge our assumptions and reveal the incredible diversity of dinosaur life. As paleontologists continue to uncover new evidence, our knowledge of these ancient creatures will undoubtedly continue to grow.

Chapter 2: Dinosaur Evolution and Adaptation

From Tiny Creatures to Gigantic Beasts

Dinosaurs didn't start out as the colossal creatures we often imagine. Their journey from small, humble beginnings to some of the largest animals ever to walk the Earth is a fascinating tale of evolution, driven by adaptation, competition, and survival. In this chapter, we'll explore how dinosaurs evolved over millions of years, adapting to their environments in remarkable ways and becoming the dominant land animals of the Mesozoic Era.

Fact 21: The First Dinosaurs Were Small and Bipedal

The earliest dinosaurs, which appeared around 230 million years ago during the late Triassic period, were relatively small and walked on two legs. These early dinosaurs, like Eoraptor and Herrerasaurus, were no larger than a modern-day dog or small horse. Their bipedal stance allowed them to move quickly, which was essential for hunting and escaping predators.

Fact 22: Dinosaurs and Crocodiles Share a Common Ancestor

Dinosaurs and modern crocodiles both belong to a group of reptiles known as archosaurs, which first appeared in the early Triassic period. Archosaurs split into two main lineages: one that led to crocodiles and another that led to dinosaurs (and eventually birds). This shared ancestry means that dinosaurs and crocodiles have some similarities, such as certain features in their skulls and ankles.

Fact 23: Dinosaurs Developed Hollow Bones for Speed and Agility

One of the key adaptations that allowed dinosaurs to thrive was the development of hollow bones. This feature made their skeletons lighter, allowing them to move more quickly and efficiently. This adaptation was especially important for theropods, the group of dinosaurs that includes Tyrannosaurus rex and Velociraptor, which relied on speed and agility to hunt their prey.

Fact 24: The Evolution of Feathers Started Before Birds

Contrary to what many people believe, feathers did not evolve exclusively for flight. In fact, feathers first appeared in dinosaurs long before the evolution of birds. Early feathers were likely used for insulation, helping small dinosaurs retain body heat. Over time, feathers became more complex and were eventually adapted for display, camouflage, and, later, flight. Fossils of dinosaurs like Sinosauropteryx show evidence of primitive feathers, indicating that this adaptation was widespread among theropods.

Fact 25: Sauropods Evolved Long Necks to Reach High Vegetation

Sauropods, the long-necked dinosaurs like Brachiosaurus and Apatosaurus, evolved their lengthy necks to reach vegetation high in trees, which allowed them to access food sources that other herbivores couldn't. This adaptation not only gave them a competitive advantage but also allowed them to grow to enormous sizes, as they had a steady supply of food. The structure of sauropods' necks was supported by lightweight, air-filled vertebrae, making it easier for them to hold up their massive heads and necks.

Fact 26: Dinosaurs Evolved Unique Teeth for Different Diets

Dinosaurs developed a wide variety of teeth adapted to their diets. Herbivorous dinosaurs, such as Triceratops and Hadrosaurus, had flat, grinding teeth that allowed them to chew tough plant material. Carnivorous dinosaurs, like Allosaurus and T. rex, had sharp, serrated teeth designed to tear through flesh. Some dinosaurs, like the duck-billed Hadrosaurus, even had hundreds of teeth in their jaws, which were constantly replaced throughout their lives.

Fact 27: Armor and Defensive Adaptations Were Common Among Dinosaurs

Many dinosaurs evolved armor and other defensive adaptations to protect themselves from predators. Ankylosaurs, for example, had bony plates embedded in their skin and wielded club-like tails that could deliver powerful blows. Stegosaurus had large, bony plates along its back and a spiked tail known as a "thagomizer," which it used for defense. These adaptations helped herbivorous dinosaurs survive in a world full of predators.

Fact 28: Some Dinosaurs Evolved Beaks for Specialized Feeding

Over time, some dinosaurs evolved beaks, which allowed them to specialize in different types of feeding. For example, ceratopsians like Triceratops had parrot-like beaks that were well-suited for clipping tough vegetation. Ornithomimosaurs, which resembled modern ostriches, had beaks that helped them eat a variety of foods, including plants and small animals. The evolution of beaks was a significant adaptation that allowed these dinosaurs to exploit different ecological niches.

Fact 29: Theropods Evolved Into Birds

One of the most significant evolutionary events in the history of dinosaurs was the evolution of birds from small, feathered theropods. This transition occurred gradually over millions of years, with each generation of theropods developing more bird-like features, such as feathers, wishbones, and eventually, the ability to fly. Archaeopteryx, which lived around 150 million years ago, is often cited as one of the earliest known birds, showcasing a mix of dinosaur and avian characteristics.

Fact 30: Some Dinosaurs Grew Gigantic to Avoid Predators

One of the most remarkable aspects of dinosaur evolution is the sheer size of some species. Sauropods, in particular, evolved to grow to enormous sizes, with some species reaching lengths of over 100 feet and weights of more than 100 tons. One theory suggests that their massive size helped them avoid predation, as few predators would be capable of attacking such large animals. Additionally, their size allowed them to consume vast amounts of vegetation, ensuring a steady energy supply.

Fact 31: Dinosaur Skin Colors and Patterns Were Likely Highly Varied

While we can't know for certain what colors and patterns dinosaurs had, recent fossil discoveries have provided some clues. For example, fossilized pigments found in the feathers of some dinosaurs suggest they may have had colorful plumage similar to modern birds. Other fossils show evidence of scales and skin patterns, indicating that dinosaurs had a wide range of appearances. This diversity in skin color and patterns likely played a role in camouflage, mating displays, and species recognition.

Fact 32: Dinosaurs Evolved Complex Social Behaviors

There is growing evidence that many dinosaurs lived in complex social groups and exhibited behaviors similar to those of modern animals. Fossilized trackways suggest that some dinosaurs traveled in herds, while others, like the ceratopsians, may have lived in family groups. Evidence of nesting sites, such as those of the Maiasaura, indicates that some dinosaurs cared for their young, building nests and protecting their eggs. These social behaviors were important adaptations that helped dinosaurs survive in a world full of challenges.

Fact 33: Dinosaurs Evolved Crests and Horns for Display and Defense

Many dinosaurs developed elaborate crests, horns, and frills, which served a variety of functions. In ceratopsians like Triceratops, the large frill and horns were likely used for defense against predators, as well as for display during mating rituals. Hadrosaurs, such as Parasaurolophus, had hollow crests that may have been used to produce sounds, helping them communicate with others in their group. These adaptations show how dinosaurs used physical features to enhance their chances of survival and reproduction.

Fact 34: Dinosaurs Evolved Efficient Respiratory Systems

Dinosaurs, particularly theropods and sauropods, evolved highly efficient respiratory systems that helped them sustain their large bodies and active lifestyles. Evidence suggests that many dinosaurs had a system of air sacs similar to modern birds, which allowed them to take in more oxygen with each breath. This adaptation was crucial for sustaining the high levels of activity needed for hunting, foraging, and evading predators.

Fact 35: Some Dinosaurs Evolved to Run at High Speeds

Speed was a critical adaptation for both predators and prey in the dinosaur world. Theropods like Velociraptor and Ornithomimus had long, slender legs that allowed them to run at high speeds, helping them chase down prey or escape danger. Fossil evidence, such as footprints and leg bone structure, suggests that some dinosaurs could reach speeds of 25 to 40 miles per hour, making them formidable hunters and agile escape artists.

Fact 36: Dinosaurs Evolved Specialized Claws for Different Functions

The claws of dinosaurs were highly specialized, evolving in different shapes and sizes to suit various functions. Theropods like Deinonychus had large, sickle-shaped claws on their feet, which they used to slash and grip prey. Herbivorous dinosaurs like Iguanodon had thumb spikes that may have been used for defense. Some dinosaurs, like the therizinosaurs, had long, curved claws that were likely used for feeding on vegetation. These adaptations highlight the diversity of dinosaur lifestyles and feeding strategies.

Fact 37: Some Dinosaurs Evolved to Swim and Hunt in Water

While most dinosaurs were land-dwellers, some species adapted to life in aquatic environments. Spinosaurus, for example, had a long, crocodile-like snout, conical teeth, and paddle-like limbs, which suggest it was well adapted for hunting fish in rivers and lakes. This adaptation is rare among dinosaurs, but it shows the incredible versatility of these creatures as they evolved to occupy various ecological niches.

Fact 38: The Evolution of Herding Behaviors Provided Safety in Numbers

Many herbivorous dinosaurs, such as hadrosaurs and ceratopsians, evolved to live in herds. This social behavior provided protection from predators, as there is safety in numbers. Fossil evidence, including trackways and bone beds, indicates that these dinosaurs traveled together, foraged in groups, and may have even coordinated their movements to avoid danger. Herding also facilitated communication and mating, which were essential for the survival of these species.

Fact 39: Dinosaurs Evolved Tail Adaptations for Balance and Defense

Dinosaur tails were not just for show—they were vital for balance, especially in bipedal species. Theropods like Tyrannosaurus rex used their tails as counterbalances while running or hunting, allowing them to make quick turns and maintain stability. Other dinosaurs, like the ankylosaurs, evolved heavy, club-like tails that could be swung as weapons against predators. The tail was a versatile appendage that played a crucial role in the survival of many dinosaur species.

Fact 40: Some Dinosaurs Evolved to Survive Harsh Climates

Dinosaurs lived in a wide range of environments, from lush forests to arid deserts. Some species evolved to survive in harsh climates, developing adaptations to cope with extreme temperatures, limited water, and scarce food. For example, some desert-dwelling dinosaurs, like the small theropod Coelophysis, may have been able to conserve water and survive on a diet of small animals and insects. In colder climates, feathered dinosaurs like Yutyrannus may have used their plumage for insulation, helping them retain body heat in icy conditions.

Fact 41: The Evolution of Different Egg-Laying Strategies

Dinosaurs, like modern reptiles and birds, laid eggs, but their egg-laying strategies varied widely. Some dinosaurs, like the hadrosaurs, laid their eggs in large communal nests, which they guarded and tended until the eggs hatched. Others, like the sauropods, laid their eggs in isolated nests and left them to incubate on their own. The size, shape, and structure of dinosaur eggs also varied, with some species producing eggs as large as a basketball and others laying eggs no bigger than a tennis ball. These reproductive strategies were critical for the survival of dinosaur species in different environments.

Fact 42: Some Dinosaurs Evolved Camouflage to Evade Predators

Camouflage was an important adaptation for many dinosaurs, particularly for those that were preyed upon by larger carnivores. Fossil evidence, including the discovery of fossilized skin and feathers, suggests that some dinosaurs had patterns and colors that helped them blend into their surroundings. This adaptation allowed them to avoid detection by predators, increasing their chances of survival. For example, the small theropod Sinosauropteryx is believed to have had a striped tail, which may have served as camouflage in its environment.

Fact 43: The Evolution of Gigantothermy in Large Dinosaurs

Gigantothermy, also known as "bulk homeothermy," is a concept that explains how large dinosaurs maintained a relatively stable internal temperature. Due to their massive size, large dinosaurs like sauropods could retain heat more effectively than smaller animals, reducing the need for active thermoregulation. This adaptation allowed them to thrive in a variety of climates, from tropical forests to cooler regions, by maintaining a constant body temperature despite external fluctuations.

Fact 44: Dinosaurs Evolved Sensory Adaptations for Survival

Dinosaurs developed a range of sensory adaptations to help them find food, evade predators, and navigate their environments. For example, theropods like

Tyrannosaurus rex had forward-facing eyes, which gave them binocular vision and improved depth perception—a critical adaptation for hunting. Some herbivorous dinosaurs, like the hadrosaurs, had large nasal passages that may have enhanced their sense of smell, helping them locate food or detect predators. These sensory adaptations played a crucial role in the survival and success of dinosaurs.

Fact 45: Dinosaurs Evolved to Communicate with Each Other

Communication was key to the social lives of many dinosaurs. Fossil evidence suggests that some dinosaurs, like the hadrosaurs, could produce vocalizations using their crests, which may have acted as resonating chambers. These sounds could have been used to attract mates, warn of danger, or coordinate group movements. Other dinosaurs, like ceratopsians, may have used visual signals, such as the display of their frills and horns, to communicate with each other. These communication strategies were vital for maintaining social bonds and ensuring the survival of the species.

Fact 46: Dinosaurs Evolved Diverse Reproductive Strategies

Dinosaurs exhibited a wide range of reproductive strategies, from the number of eggs they laid to how they cared for their young. Some species, like the theropod Oviraptor, are believed to have incubated their eggs by sitting on their nests, similar to modern birds. Others, like the sauropods, may have laid dozens of eggs at once, relying on sheer numbers to ensure that some would survive. These diverse reproductive strategies allowed dinosaurs to adapt to different environments and increase their chances of passing on their genes to the next generation.

Fact 47: The Evolution of Specialized Feeding Adaptations

Different groups of dinosaurs evolved specialized feeding adaptations that allowed them to exploit a variety of food sources. For example, the long-necked sauropods evolved to browse high vegetation, while the duck-billed hadrosaurs developed a complex set of teeth for grinding tough plant material. Carnivorous dinosaurs, like the theropods, evolved sharp, serrated teeth and strong jaws for tearing flesh. These adaptations allowed dinosaurs to occupy a wide range of ecological niches and contributed to their success as a group.

Fact 48: Dinosaurs Evolved to Survive in Diverse Habitats

Dinosaurs were incredibly adaptable, evolving to live in a wide range of habitats across the globe. From dense forests to arid deserts, dinosaurs developed the necessary adaptations to thrive in different environments. For example, the small theropod Velociraptor lived in the arid deserts of what is now Mongolia, while the giant sauropod Argentinosaurus roamed the lush, forested plains of South America. This adaptability was a key factor in the widespread success of dinosaurs during the Mesozoic Era.

Fact 49: The Evolution of Symbiotic Relationships with Plants

Some dinosaurs developed symbiotic relationships with plants, helping to shape the ecosystems in which they lived. For example, large herbivorous dinosaurs like sauropods may have played a role in the dispersal of plant seeds, as they consumed vast amounts of vegetation and excreted seeds across large areas. In return, these plants provided a steady food source for the dinosaurs. This mutually beneficial relationship helped maintain the balance of ecosystems during the age of dinosaurs.

Fact 50: Dinosaurs Adapted to Changing Environments Over Time

The Mesozoic Era was a time of significant environmental change, with shifting continents, fluctuating climates, and evolving ecosystems. Dinosaurs had to continuously adapt to these changes to survive. Some species, like the adaptable hadrosaurs, thrived in a variety of environments, while others, like the specialized sauropods, faced challenges as their preferred habitats changed. The ability to adapt to new environments was a crucial factor in the success and longevity of dinosaurs during their reign.

Chapter 3: Types of Dinosaurs

The Giants, the Terrifying, and the Peculiar

Dinosaurs came in an incredible variety of shapes and sizes, from tiny, bird-like creatures to enormous, lumbering giants. In this chapter, we'll delve into the different types of dinosaurs, exploring the major groups, their defining characteristics, and some of the most iconic species that have captured our imaginations.

Fact 51: Dinosaurs are Divided into Two Major Groups

Dinosaurs are traditionally divided into two major groups based on the structure of their hips: the Saurischia and the Ornithischia. Saurischians, meaning "lizard-hipped," include the theropods (bipedal carnivores) and sauropodomorphs (long-necked herbivores). Ornithischians, meaning "bird-hipped," include a variety of herbivorous dinosaurs, such as stegosaurs, ankylosaurs, and ceratopsians. Despite their name, the bird-hipped dinosaurs are not the ancestors of modern birds—those actually evolved from the lizard-hipped theropods.

Fact 52: Theropods Were the Dominant Predators

Theropods were a group of bipedal, mostly carnivorous dinosaurs that ranged from the tiny Compsognathus to the massive Tyrannosaurus rex. They had sharp, serrated teeth, powerful jaws, and claws designed for hunting. Theropods were among the most successful dinosaur groups, with members living on every continent and evolving into a wide range of forms, including the ancestors of modern birds.

Fact 53: Sauropods Were the Largest Land Animals Ever

Sauropods, the long-necked giants of the dinosaur world, were the largest land animals to ever exist. Species like Argentinosaurus and Patagotitan reached lengths of over 100 feet and weights of more than 70 tons. Sauropods were herbivores, using their long necks to reach vegetation high in trees. Their massive size likely helped protect them from predators, and their column-like legs supported their immense weight.

Fact 54: Ceratopsians Were Known for Their Impressive Horns and Frills

Ceratopsians, or "horned dinosaurs," are best known for their distinctive facial horns and large frills. Triceratops is the most famous member of this group, with its three facial horns and bony frill. These features were likely used for defense, as well as for display during mating rituals. Other ceratopsians, like Styracosaurus and Pentaceratops, had even more elaborate horns and frills, showcasing the diversity within this group.

Fact 55: Hadrosaurs Were the "Duck-Billed" Dinosaurs

Hadrosaurs, commonly known as "duck-billed" dinosaurs, were a group of herbivorous dinosaurs known for their broad, flat beaks. They were among the most successful dinosaurs of the late Cretaceous period, with species like Edmontosaurus and Parasaurolophus spread across North America and Asia. Hadrosaurs had complex teeth designed for grinding tough plant material, and some species had elaborate crests on their heads that may have been used for communication.

Fact 56: Stegosaurs Had Plates and Spikes for Protection

Stegosaurs were a group of herbivorous dinosaurs characterized by the distinctive plates and spikes along their backs and tails. Stegosaurus, the most famous member of this group, had two rows of large, bony plates along its back and a spiked tail, known as a thagomizer, which it likely used for defense. Despite their formidable appearance, stegosaurs had relatively small brains and were slow-moving, relying on their armor for protection.

Fact 57: Ankylosaurs Were the "Tanks" of the Dinosaur World

Ankylosaurs were heavily armored dinosaurs, often described as the "tanks" of the dinosaur world. They were covered in thick, bony plates and had club-like tails that they could swing at predators. Ankylosaurus, one of the largest and most well-known ankylosaurs, was built like a living fortress, with armor that protected it from the sharp teeth and claws of theropod predators like Tyrannosaurus rex.

Fact 58: Pterosaurs Were Not Dinosaurs, but Close Relatives

While often associated with dinosaurs, pterosaurs were not actually dinosaurs but close relatives. These flying reptiles lived alongside dinosaurs and were the first vertebrates to achieve powered flight. Pterosaurs ranged from the small, sparrow-sized Nemicolopterus to the enormous Quetzalcoatlus, which had a wingspan of up to 40 feet. They filled various ecological niches, from fish-eating predators to scavengers.

Fact 59: Prosauropods Were the Early Relatives of Sauropods

Prosauropods were early relatives of the giant sauropods and were among the first large herbivorous dinosaurs. They lived during the late Triassic and early Jurassic periods and were characterized by their long necks and relatively small size compared to their later sauropod descendants. Plateosaurus is one of the best-known prosauropods, reaching lengths of up to 30 feet. Prosauropods walked on two or four legs and fed on vegetation low to the ground.

Fact 60: Ornithomimosaurs Resembled Modern Ostriches

Ornithomimosaurs, often called "ostrich dinosaurs," were theropods that resembled modern ostriches in both appearance and behavior. They were fast, bipedal dinosaurs with long legs, small heads, and beak-like mouths. Ornithomimus is a well-known member of this group, known for its speed and agility. These dinosaurs were likely omnivorous, feeding on a diet of plants, small animals, and insects.

Fact 61: Dromaeosaurs Were the "Raptors" of the Dinosaur World

Dromaeosaurs, often referred to as "raptors," were a group of small to medium-sized theropods known for their agility, intelligence, and sharp, sickle-shaped claws. Velociraptor and Deinonychus are the most famous dromaeosaurs, popularized by movies like "Jurassic Park." These dinosaurs were likely pack hunters, using their claws and speed to take down prey. Some dromaeosaurs had feathers, suggesting a close evolutionary relationship with birds.

Fact 62: Spinosaurids Were Aquatic Hunters

Spinosaurids were a group of theropods adapted for a semi-aquatic lifestyle. They had long, crocodile-like snouts filled with conical teeth, ideal for catching fish. Spinosaurus, the largest and most famous spinosaurid, could reach lengths of over 50 feet and had a distinctive sail on its back. Spinosaurids lived in river and lake environments, where they hunted fish and other aquatic prey.

Fact 63: Pachycephalosaurs Had Domed Skulls for Head-Butting

Pachycephalosaurs, or "thick-headed lizards," were herbivorous dinosaurs known for their thick, domed skulls. These skulls, which could be up to 10 inches thick, were likely used in head-butting contests, either for dominance within the group or during mating rituals. Pachycephalosaurus is the most well-known member of this group, with a skull that was perfectly adapted for impact.

Fact 64: Iguanodonts Were Early Cretaceous Herbivores

Iguanodonts were a group of herbivorous dinosaurs that lived during the early Cretaceous period. They were among the first dinosaurs to be discovered and scientifically described. Iguanodon, the namesake of the group, was a large herbivore with a spiked thumb, which it may have used for defense. Iguanodonts walked on both two and four legs and were well-adapted for grazing on low vegetation.

Fact 65: Titanosaurs Were the Last of the Sauropods

Titanosaurs were the last surviving group of sauropods, living during the late Cretaceous period. They were widespread, with fossils found on every continent, including Antarctica. Titanosaurs were some of the largest dinosaurs, with species like Argentinosaurus and Dreadnoughtus reaching massive sizes. Unlike their earlier relatives, titanosaurs had broader bodies and sometimes featured armored skin.

Fact 66: Therizinosaurs Had Large Claws and Were Herbivorous Theropods

Therizinosaurs were a group of theropods with long, scythe-like claws and herbivorous diets, a rarity among theropods. These dinosaurs had a peculiar appearance, with small heads, potbellies, and large claws on their forelimbs. Therizinosaurus is the most well-known member of this group, with claws that could reach lengths of up to three feet. Despite their fearsome claws, therizinosaurs were peaceful plant-eaters, using their claws to pull down branches or strip leaves.

Fact 67: Ankylosaurids and Nodosaurids Were Heavily Armored Relatives

The Ankylosauria group is divided into two main families: ankylosaurids and nodosaurids. Ankylosaurids, like Ankylosaurus, had tail clubs and extensive body armor, while nodosaurids, like Edmontonia, had less extensive armor and no tail clubs. Both families were heavily built and well-protected against predators, with nodosaurids often having spikes or ridges along their backs and sides for added defense.

Fact 68: Marginocephalians Included Both Ceratopsians and Pachycephalosaurs

The Marginocephalia clade includes both ceratopsians (like Triceratops) and pachycephalosaurs (like Pachycephalosaurus). These dinosaurs are characterized by the presence of a shelf or frill at the back of their skulls. While ceratopsians used their frills and horns for defense and display, pachycephalosaurs likely used their domed skulls for head-butting. This diverse group of herbivores showcases the wide range of adaptations that dinosaurs developed.

Fact 69: Nothosaurs Were Marine Reptiles, Not Dinosaurs

Nothosaurs were marine reptiles that lived during the Triassic period, long before the heyday of the dinosaurs. They were not dinosaurs but lived alongside early dinosaurs in the seas. Nothosaurs had long necks, streamlined bodies, and flipper-like limbs, making them well-suited for hunting fish. They are considered early relatives of plesiosaurs, another group of marine reptiles that thrived in the later Mesozoic seas.

Fact 70: Abelisaurids Were Southern Hemisphere Predators

Abelisaurids were a group of theropods that lived primarily in the southern continents, including South America, Africa, and India, during the late Cretaceous period. They were characterized by their short, deep skulls and tiny, often useless forearms. Carnotaurus is the most famous abelisaurid, known for its distinctive horns and fast, agile build. These dinosaurs were top predators in their ecosystems, filling the niche occupied by tyrannosaurs in the Northern Hemisphere.

Fact 71: Hadrosaurids Had Complex Dental Batteries

Hadrosaurids, or duck-billed dinosaurs, had some of the most complex dental arrangements of any dinosaur. They possessed dental batteries, which were rows of tightly packed teeth that formed a continuous grinding surface. These teeth were ideal for processing tough plant material, allowing hadrosaurids to efficiently chew their food before swallowing. This adaptation made them highly successful herbivores during the late Cretaceous period.

Fact 72: Oviraptorosaurs Were Egg-Thieving or Protective Parents?

Oviraptorosaurs were a group of feathered theropods known for their unusual beak-like jaws and sometimes elaborate crests. The name "Oviraptor," meaning "egg thief," was given based on the belief that these dinosaurs stole and ate eggs. However, further evidence suggests that they were actually caring parents who guarded their nests. Fossils of Oviraptor with eggs have been found, indicating that these dinosaurs may have been brooding their clutches, similar to modern birds.

Fact 73: Protoceratopsids Were Small, Horned Dinosaurs

Protoceratopsids were small, horned dinosaurs that lived during the late Cretaceous period. They are considered the ancestors of larger ceratopsians like Triceratops. Protoceratops, the most famous member of this group, was about the size of a large dog and had a small frill and beak, but no horns. These dinosaurs lived in herds and were likely prey for larger theropods, as evidenced by fossils showing signs of predation.

Fact 74: Troodontids Were Small, Bird-Like Dinosaurs with Large Brains

Troodontids were a group of small, bird-like theropods known for their large brains relative to body size, suggesting they were among the more intelligent dinosaurs. Troodon is the most well-known member of this group, recognized by its large eyes, which suggest it may have been nocturnal. Troodontids had long, slender limbs and were likely agile hunters or omnivores, feeding on small animals, insects, and plants.

Fact 75: Psittacosaurs Were Early Horned Dinosaurs with Parrot-Like Beaks

Psittacosaurs were small, early horned dinosaurs that lived during the early Cretaceous period. They are named for their parrot-like beaks, which were used to clip and chew tough vegetation. Psittacosaurus, the best-known member of this group, had a set of long bristles on its tail, which may have been used for display or communication. These dinosaurs were likely the ancestors of later, larger ceratopsians.

Fact 76: Hypsilophodonts Were Small, Agile Herbivores

Hypsilophodonts were a group of small, bipedal herbivores that lived during the Jurassic and Cretaceous periods. They were characterized by their long legs and tails, which made them fast and agile runners. Hypsilophodon, one of the more famous members of this group, was about the size of a dog and likely lived in forests, feeding on low-lying vegetation. These dinosaurs were well-adapted to a life of constant movement, helping them avoid predators.

Fact 77: Alvarezsaurids Were Small, Insectivorous Dinosaurs with Tiny Arms

Alvarezsaurids were a group of small, bipedal dinosaurs with very short, but powerful, arms. These dinosaurs, like Alvarezsaurus and Mononykus, are believed to have been insectivores, using their specialized arms to dig into termite mounds or rotting wood to extract insects. Their tiny arms had large claws, making them highly specialized for their niche, despite their unusual appearance.

Fact 78: Thalattosaurs Were Marine Reptiles, Not Dinosaurs

Thalattosaurs were marine reptiles that lived during the Triassic period, sharing the oceans with early dinosaurs. They were not dinosaurs but were related to the ancestors of modern lizards and snakes. Thalattosaurs had elongated bodies, paddle-like limbs, and long tails that helped them swim through the water. Their diet likely consisted of fish and other marine creatures, making them important predators in their ecosystems.

Fact 79: Diplodocids Were Long-Necked Sauropods with Whip-Like Tails

Diplodocids were a family of sauropods known for their extremely long necks and tails. Diplodocus, the most famous member, could reach lengths of over 80 feet, with nearly half of that length being its neck and tail. These dinosaurs likely used their tails as whips, either for defense or communication. Diplodocids were herbivores, using their long necks to reach vegetation that other dinosaurs couldn't access.

Fact 80: Theropods Included Both Giant Predators and Tiny Feathered Dinosaurs

Theropods, the group that includes famous giants like Tyrannosaurus rex, also included many smaller, feathered dinosaurs. While the larger theropods were apex predators, the smaller ones occupied a variety of ecological niches, from insectivores to omnivores. This diversity within the theropod group showcases the wide range of adaptations that allowed these dinosaurs to thrive in different environments.

Fact 81: Sauropterygians Were Marine Reptiles, Not Dinosaurs

Sauropterygians were marine reptiles that lived during the Mesozoic era, alongside dinosaurs. They were not dinosaurs but shared the seas with them. This group includes the plesiosaurs, known for their long necks and paddle-like limbs. Sauropterygians were adapted to life in the ocean, with some species growing to impressive sizes and becoming top predators in their marine environments.

Fact 82: Titanosaurs Were the Last Giant Sauropods

Titanosaurs were the last and among the largest of the sauropods, living during the late Cretaceous period. These massive herbivores, such as Argentinosaurus and Patagotitan, were spread across the continents and represent some of the largest land animals to have ever lived. Unlike earlier sauropods, titanosaurs had wider bodies and often sported bony armor, making them both massive and well-protected.

Fact 83: The Hypsilophodonts Were Fast, Agile Dinosaurs

Hypsilophodonts were small, agile dinosaurs that lived during the Jurassic and Cretaceous periods. They were bipedal herbivores with long legs and tails, adapted for fast running. These dinosaurs likely used their speed to evade predators and may have lived in groups for added protection. Their small size and agility made them some of the more adaptable dinosaurs in their ecosystems.

Fact 84: Megaraptorans Were Large, Lightly-Built Predators

Megaraptorans were a group of large theropods characterized by their long arms and large claws. Despite their name, they were not closely related to the dromaeosaurs ("raptors") but were instead a distinct group of lightly-built, agile predators. Megaraptor, the namesake of the group, had massive claws on its hands, which it likely used to catch and subdue prey. These dinosaurs were fast and nimble, making them effective hunters.

Fact 85: Ceratopsians Evolved from Small, Bipedal Ancestors

Ceratopsians, the horned dinosaurs like Triceratops, evolved from small, bipedal ancestors that lived during the early Cretaceous period. These early ceratopsians, such as Psittacosaurus, were much smaller than their later relatives and lacked the large horns and frills. Over time, ceratopsians evolved to become larger and more heavily armored, with the iconic frills and horns that characterize the group.

Fact 86: Rebbachisaurids Were Sauropods with Unique Neck Spines

Rebbachisaurids were a group of sauropods known for their unique neck vertebrae, which had long, thin spines. These dinosaurs lived during the mid to late Cretaceous period and were found primarily in South America and Africa. Rebbachisaurids, like Nigersaurus, had broad, flat snouts and were likely low-browsing herbivores. Their unique neck structure suggests they had a different feeding strategy compared to other sauropods.

Fact 87: Titanosaurs Had Different Leg and Body Structures Compared to Earlier Sauropods

Titanosaurs, the last of the giant sauropods, had distinct body and leg structures compared to their earlier relatives. Unlike earlier sauropods, titanosaurs had wider, more robust bodies and legs, which supported their massive size. They also had more flexible necks, allowing them to reach a wider range of vegetation. These adaptations made titanosaurs some of the most successful sauropods during the late Cretaceous period.

Fact 88: The Ornithopods Were a Diverse Group of Herbivorous Dinosaurs

Ornithopods were a diverse group of herbivorous dinosaurs that included both small, fast runners and large, duck-billed dinosaurs. They were characterized by their beaks and grinding teeth, which allowed them to process tough plant material. Ornithopods were highly successful, with members like Iguanodon and Hadrosaurus thriving in different environments across the globe.

Fact 89: Plateosaurs Were Early Sauropodomorphs

Plateosaurs were among the earliest sauropodomorphs, the group that eventually gave rise to the giant sauropods. They lived during the late Triassic and early Jurassic periods and were characterized by their long necks and tails. Plateosaurus, one of the most well-known members, was a large herbivore that walked on two or four legs. These dinosaurs were some of the first to adopt a fully herbivorous diet, setting the stage for the later evolution of sauropods.

Fact 90: Nodosaurids Lacked Tail Clubs but Had Spiky Armor

Nodosaurids were a family of armored dinosaurs related to ankylosaurs, but unlike their relatives, they lacked tail clubs. Instead, nodosaurids had rows of spikes and bony plates along their backs and sides, which provided protection from predators. These dinosaurs were herbivores and likely used their armor to deter attacks while they foraged for plants.

Chapter 4: Dinosaur Behavior and Social Structure

How Dinosaurs Lived, Fought, and Roamed

Understanding dinosaur behavior is like piecing together a giant prehistoric puzzle. Although we can never directly observe how dinosaurs acted, paleontologists have uncovered fascinating clues through fossils, footprints, and even rare evidence of social interactions. In this chapter, we'll explore the behaviors that defined dinosaur life—from hunting and socializing to nesting and migration.

Fact 91: Dinosaurs Lived in Herds, Packs, and Solitary Lives

Dinosaurs exhibited a wide range of social behaviors. Some species, like the massive sauropods, likely traveled in herds for protection, with fossilized trackways showing groups moving together. On the other hand, solitary behaviors were also common, especially among larger predators like Tyrannosaurus rex, which may have lived and hunted alone. Raptors like Velociraptor might have hunted in packs, using teamwork to take down larger prey.

Fact 92: Dinosaurs Communicated Using Vocalizations and Visual Displays

While we can't hear what dinosaurs sounded like, evidence suggests that many species communicated through vocalizations and visual displays. Dinosaurs like Parasaurolophus had hollow crests that may have acted as resonating chambers, allowing them to produce distinctive calls. Ceratopsians, with their elaborate frills and horns, likely used visual signals for communication, possibly during mating rituals or territorial disputes.

Fact 93: The Fossil Record Shows Evidence of Dinosaur Migration

Some dinosaurs, particularly large herbivores, may have migrated seasonally in search of food. Fossilized trackways provide evidence of these movements, showing groups of dinosaurs traveling long distances. Isotopic analysis of dinosaur teeth also supports the idea of migration, revealing changes in diet and water sources that align with seasonal shifts. These migrations would have been essential for survival, especially in areas with harsh climates.

Fact 94: Dinosaurs Engaged in Complex Courtship Behaviors

Courtship in dinosaurs likely involved elaborate displays, much like modern birds and reptiles. For instance, some theropods may have used their feathers in mating dances or displays, while ceratopsians might have clashed horns in battles for dominance. Evidence of these behaviors comes from fossils showing healed injuries, which suggests that dinosaurs engaged in fights over mates or territory.

Fact 95: Dinosaurs Built Nests and Cared for Their Young

Nesting behaviors in dinosaurs were surprisingly complex. Fossilized nests and eggs provide evidence that many species, like the hadrosaur Maiasaura, built nests and cared for their young. These dinosaurs laid their eggs in carefully constructed nests and may have guarded them until they hatched. Some species, like Oviraptor, are even thought to have incubated their eggs by sitting on them, similar to modern birds.

Fact 96: Dinosaurs Displayed Parental Care

Parental care in dinosaurs wasn't limited to nesting. Some species likely took care of their young long after they hatched. Fossil sites containing juveniles alongside adults suggest that these dinosaurs lived in family groups, where parents protected and possibly even fed their offspring. Maiasaura, whose name means "good mother lizard," is one of the most famous examples of a dinosaur that likely cared for its young.

Fact 97: Evidence Suggests Some Dinosaurs Were Social Animals

Fossil evidence, including trackways and bone beds, suggests that some dinosaurs lived in social groups. Hadrosaurs, for example, are often found in large bone beds, indicating they may have lived in herds. These social structures provided protection against predators and made it easier to find food. Living in groups also likely played a role in the success of these dinosaurs, allowing them to thrive in a variety of environments.

Fact 98: Dinosaurs Used Their Tails for Balance and Defense

Tails were an essential part of a dinosaur's anatomy, serving multiple purposes. For bipedal dinosaurs, like theropods, the tail acted as a counterbalance, helping them maintain stability while running or hunting. For others, like the armored ankylosaurs, the tail evolved into a formidable weapon, capable of delivering powerful blows to predators. The versatility of the tail highlights its importance in dinosaur behavior and survival.

Fact 99: Many Dinosaurs Were Territorial

Territorial behaviors were likely common among dinosaurs, especially carnivores. Fossils showing healed wounds suggest that dinosaurs engaged in territorial disputes, possibly over food sources or mating rights. Large predators like Allosaurus may have marked their territory and defended it against rivals, while herbivores like Triceratops might have used their horns and frills to intimidate others encroaching on their space.

Fact 100: Some Dinosaurs Showed Evidence of Cooperative Hunting

Cooperative hunting, where groups of predators work together to catch prey, may have been practiced by some theropods. Fossil evidence, including trackways and bite marks, suggests that raptors like Deinonychus hunted in packs, using their numbers to overwhelm larger prey. This behavior would have given these dinosaurs a significant advantage, allowing them to take down animals much larger than themselves.

Fact 101: Dinosaurs Had Display Structures for Mating Rituals

Many dinosaurs evolved elaborate display structures, like crests, horns, and frills, which were likely used during mating rituals. These features may have signaled fitness to potential mates or been used in combat between rivals. The brightly colored feathers of some theropods, as suggested by fossil evidence, also likely played a role in courtship, similar to how modern birds use plumage to attract mates.

Fact 102: Dinosaur Herds Could Have Reached Massive Sizes

Some dinosaur herds, particularly those of large herbivores like sauropods, may have reached enormous sizes. Fossil trackways suggest that these herds could have included hundreds or even thousands of individuals, moving together across the landscape. These massive groups would have provided safety in numbers, reducing the risk of predation and making it easier to find food.

Fact 103: Some Dinosaurs Exhibited Cannibalistic Behavior

Cannibalism, where a species feeds on its own kind, is believed to have occurred among some dinosaurs. Fossil evidence, such as bite marks on bones from the same species, suggests that dinosaurs like Majungasaurus may have practiced cannibalism, especially in times of food scarcity. This behavior, while rare, highlights the harsh realities of life in the prehistoric world.

Fact 104: Dinosaurs May Have Engaged in Seasonal Migration

Seasonal migration is believed to have been a common behavior among certain dinosaurs, particularly those living in regions with significant climate variations. As seasons changed, these dinosaurs would have migrated to areas with more abundant food and better living conditions. Fossil evidence, such as changes in tooth enamel isotopes, supports the idea that dinosaurs like sauropods undertook long migrations.

Fact 105: Dinosaurs Used Vocalizations to Communicate

Vocalizations likely played a key role in dinosaur communication, particularly for social species. While we don't have direct evidence of dinosaur sounds, the structure of some dinosaur skulls suggests they could produce a range of noises. Hadrosaurs, with their resonating crests, may have produced deep, trumpet-like calls, while smaller theropods might have used high-pitched screeches to communicate.

Fact 106: Dinosaur Fights Were Likely Common During Mating Season

Mating season would have been a time of intense competition among dinosaurs, particularly males vying for the attention of females. Fossil evidence, such as scars and healed wounds, indicates that dinosaurs engaged in physical confrontations, using their horns, claws, and teeth to fight rivals. These battles could be fierce, with the winners earning the right to mate and pass on their genes.

Fact 107: Some Dinosaurs Exhibited Altruistic Behaviors

There is evidence to suggest that some dinosaurs exhibited altruistic behaviors, where individuals would act to benefit the group, even at a personal cost. For example, in some species, older or weaker members of a herd may have positioned themselves on the outskirts, providing a buffer against predators for the younger, more vulnerable members. This kind of behavior would have strengthened social bonds and increased the overall survival rate of the group.

Fact 108: Fossil Evidence Suggests Dinosaurs Had Complex Social Hierarchies

Dinosaurs that lived in groups likely had complex social hierarchies, similar to those seen in modern animals. Dominance hierarchies would have determined access to resources like food and mates. Fossil evidence, such as bite marks and injuries, suggests that these hierarchies were established through physical confrontations. In species like the ceratopsians, dominance might have been displayed through the size and shape of frills and horns.

Fact 109: Dinosaurs Used Tools in Their Environment

While not in the same way as modern primates, some dinosaurs might have used natural objects in their environment as tools. For instance, it's possible that certain dinosaurs used rocks or other hard surfaces to break open tough-shelled prey, such as mollusks. This behavior would have required a level of intelligence and problem-solving ability that we typically associate with more modern animals.

Fact 110: Dinosaur Tracks Provide Insights into Behavior and Movement

Fossilized dinosaur tracks, also known as ichnites, offer a wealth of information about how dinosaurs moved and interacted with their environment. These tracks can reveal whether a dinosaur was running, walking, or even limping.

They can also show group behavior, such as herding or hunting. By studying trackways, paleontologists can reconstruct the behavior and dynamics of dinosaur communities.

Fact 111: Some Dinosaurs Showed Signs of Play Behavior

Play behavior, which is common in many modern animals, may have also been present in dinosaurs. Evidence for this comes from the discovery of fossilized trackways that suggest dinosaurs were not always moving with a clear purpose, such as foraging or migrating. These tracks show patterns that could indicate playful behavior, such as chasing or mock-fighting, particularly among juveniles.

Fact 112: Dinosaurs May Have Displayed Mourning Behavior

There is some speculation that dinosaurs, particularly social species, may have exhibited mourning behaviors when a member of their group died. While direct evidence is lacking, the strong social bonds seen in modern animals, such as elephants and primates, suggest that dinosaurs with similar social structures might have experienced and displayed grief.

Fact 113: Some Dinosaurs Used Camouflage for Protection

Camouflage was an important survival strategy for many dinosaurs, particularly those that were preyed upon by larger predators. Fossil evidence, such as the discovery of pigment in preserved feathers and skin, suggests that some dinosaurs had colors and patterns that helped them blend into their environment. This camouflage would have made it more difficult for predators to spot them, increasing their chances of survival.

Fact 114: Dinosaurs Had Complex Social Bonds

Complex social bonds likely existed among many dinosaur species, particularly those that lived in herds or packs. These bonds would have been essential for group cohesion and survival. Fossil evidence suggests that some dinosaurs engaged in mutual grooming, similar to the way many modern animals maintain social bonds. This behavior would have helped to strengthen relationships within the group and reduce stress.

Fact 115: Territorial Displays Included Visual and Auditory Signals

Territorial displays in dinosaurs likely included both visual and auditory signals. Large, brightly colored frills, crests, and feathers could have been used to warn off rivals or attract mates. Loud vocalizations, possibly amplified by resonating chambers in the skulls of certain species, would have served as an auditory warning to others encroaching on their territory. These displays would have been an important part of maintaining dominance and securing resources.

Fact 116: Dinosaurs Adapted Their Behavior to Changing Environments

As the Earth's climate and geography changed over millions of years, dinosaurs adapted their behavior to survive. For example, species that lived in arid environments might have developed behaviors to conserve water, such as foraging at night when it was cooler. Dinosaurs living in polar regions may have huddled together for warmth or migrated to warmer areas during the harshest months. These behavioral adaptations were crucial for the long-term survival of dinosaurs in a variety of environments.

Fact 117: Evidence Suggests Some Dinosaurs Had Mating Rituals Similar to Modern Birds

Some dinosaurs likely engaged in elaborate mating rituals similar to those seen in modern birds. Fossil evidence, such as the discovery of nests and the arrangement of eggs, suggests that dinosaurs like Oviraptor might have performed courtship displays to attract mates. These rituals could have included dances, vocalizations, and the display of feathers or other ornamental structures.

Fact 118: Dinosaurs May Have Used Tools to Build Nests

There is some evidence to suggest that certain dinosaurs used tools or natural objects to build their nests. For example, they might have used sticks or leaves to create a more comfortable or camouflaged nest. This behavior would have required a degree of intelligence and dexterity, indicating that dinosaurs were more sophisticated than we often give them credit for.

Fact 119: Dinosaurs Exhibited Signs of Emotional Intelligence

Emotional intelligence, the ability to perceive, control, and evaluate emotions, may have been present in some dinosaur species. Evidence for this comes from their complex social behaviors, such as caring for young, forming bonds with others in the group, and possibly even mourning the loss of group members. These behaviors suggest that dinosaurs had the capacity for empathy and social awareness, traits that are crucial for survival in social animals.

Fact 120: Dinosaur Behavior Was Influenced by Their Environment

The environment played a significant role in shaping dinosaur behavior. For example, dinosaurs that lived in dense forests likely developed different strategies for finding food and avoiding predators than those that lived in open plains. Environmental factors such as climate, availability of resources, and the presence of predators would have influenced everything from migration patterns to social structures.

Chapter 5: Fossil Discoveries and What They Tell Us

Unearthing the Past: From Bones to Behemoths

Fossils are the primary way we learn about dinosaurs. These ancient remnants, buried for millions of years, offer invaluable clues about how dinosaurs lived, what they looked like, and how they interacted with their environment. In this chapter, we'll explore some of the most significant fossil discoveries and what they have revealed about the lives of these fascinating creatures.

Fact 121: Fossils Form Through a Process Called Fossilization

Fossilization is a rare and complex process. When a dinosaur died, its body had to be quickly buried by sediment, such as mud, sand, or volcanic ash, to begin the fossilization process. Over millions of years, the organic materials in the bones were replaced by minerals, turning the bones into rock. Fossils can include not just bones, but also teeth, footprints, skin impressions, and even traces of feathers or fur.

Fact 122: The First Dinosaur Fossils Were Misidentified as Giants

The first recorded discovery of dinosaur fossils dates back to ancient times, when bones were often mistaken for the remains of giants or mythical creatures. It wasn't until the 19th century that scientists began to recognize these bones as belonging to a previously unknown group of reptiles. In 1824, William Buckland described Megalosaurus, the first dinosaur to be scientifically named.

Fact 123: Mary Anning's Discoveries Pioneered Paleontology

Mary Anning, a self-taught fossil collector from Lyme Regis, England, made some of the most significant early dinosaur discoveries in the early 19th century. She discovered the first complete Ichthyosaurus skeleton and the first Plesiosaurus skeleton, among other important finds. Anning's work laid the foundation for the field of paleontology and changed our understanding of prehistoric life.

Fact 124: The Bone Wars Fueled Major Dinosaur Discoveries

The late 19th century saw the rise of the "Bone Wars," a period of intense rivalry between paleontologists Othniel Charles Marsh and Edward Drinker Cope. Their competition led to the discovery of over 120 new species of dinosaurs, including some of the most famous, like Triceratops and Stegosaurus. While their methods were sometimes questionable, the Bone Wars significantly expanded our knowledge of dinosaurs.

Fact 125: Dinosaur Fossils Have Been Found on Every Continent

Dinosaur fossils have been discovered on every continent, including Antarctica. This global distribution shows that dinosaurs were incredibly adaptable, living in a wide range of environments. The discovery of fossils in Antarctica suggests that the continent was much warmer during the Mesozoic era, supporting a diverse array of dinosaur species.

Fact 126: The Largest Dinosaur Fossil Ever Found is a Titanosaur

The largest dinosaur fossil ever discovered belongs to a species of titanosaur, a group of giant sauropods that lived during the late Cretaceous period. The fossil, found in Argentina in 2014, is believed to be from a new species of titanosaur that was over 100 feet long and weighed around 70 tons. This discovery sheds light on the sheer size and scale of some of the largest dinosaurs to ever roam the Earth.

Fact 127: Fossilized Footprints Reveal Dinosaur Behavior

Fossilized footprints, also known as trackways, provide valuable insights into dinosaur behavior and movement. These footprints can show how dinosaurs walked, whether they traveled alone or in groups, and even how fast they could run. Some trackways have revealed evidence of dinosaurs interacting, such as a predator chasing prey or a group of herbivores moving together.

Fact 128: The Discovery of Dinosaur Eggs Gave Insight into Reproduction

The discovery of fossilized dinosaur eggs has provided important clues about how dinosaurs reproduced. The first dinosaur eggs were discovered in France in 1869, but it wasn't until the 1920s that paleontologists began to recognize them as such. Since then, eggs from various species have been found, revealing information about nesting behaviors, embryonic development, and parental care.

Fact 129: Fossilized Nests Show Evidence of Parental Care

Some of the most remarkable fossil discoveries are those of entire nests, complete with eggs and sometimes even fossilized embryos or hatchlings. These nests, such as those attributed to the dinosaur species Maiasaura, suggest that some dinosaurs returned to the same nesting sites year after year and cared for their young after they hatched. This evidence of parental care challenges the stereotype of dinosaurs as cold, unfeeling reptiles.

Fact 130: Soft Tissue Fossils Have Been Discovered in Dinosaur Bones

In rare cases, paleontologists have discovered soft tissues preserved within dinosaur bones. For example, in 2005, scientists found flexible tissue in the femur of a Tyrannosaurus rex, including blood vessel structures and possible remnants of cells. This discovery has opened up new avenues for research, including the possibility of extracting DNA or other biomolecules, although this remains a topic of ongoing scientific debate.

Fact 131: Fossil Feathers Confirm the Link Between Dinosaurs and Birds

The discovery of fossilized feathers in some dinosaur species, such as Archaeopteryx and Sinosauropteryx, has provided strong evidence of the evolutionary link between dinosaurs and modern birds. These feathers ranged from simple, hair-like structures to more complex, bird-like feathers. The presence of feathers in non-avian dinosaurs supports the idea that feathers originally evolved for insulation or display before being adapted for flight.

Fact 132: The First Fossilized Dinosaur Heart Was Found in a Thescelosaurus

In 2000, paleontologists discovered the first fossilized dinosaur heart in a specimen of Thescelosaurus, a small herbivorous dinosaur. The heart had a four-chambered structure, similar to that of birds and mammals, suggesting that dinosaurs may have had a more advanced circulatory system than previously thought. This discovery has important implications for our understanding of dinosaur metabolism and physiology.

Fact 133: The Liaoning Fossils Revealed the Diversity of Feathered Dinosaurs

The Liaoning Province in China has become one of the most important fossil sites in the world, particularly for its exceptionally well-preserved feathered dinosaurs. Discovered in the 1990s, the Liaoning fossils include species like Microraptor and Sinornithosaurus, which show a remarkable diversity of feather types and structures. These fossils have provided crucial evidence for the evolutionary transition from dinosaurs to birds.

Fact 134: Fossilized Skin Impressions Provide Clues About Dinosaur Appearance

In addition to bones, paleontologists have also discovered fossilized skin impressions that reveal the texture and patterning of dinosaur skin. These impressions show that many dinosaurs had scales, similar to those of modern reptiles, while others had more complex skin structures, possibly including primitive feathers. The discovery of these impressions has helped scientists reconstruct the appearance of dinosaurs with greater accuracy.

Fact 135: The Hell Creek Formation is a Treasure Trove of Late Cretaceous Fossils

The Hell Creek Formation, which spans parts of Montana, North Dakota, South Dakota, and Wyoming, is one of the most significant fossil sites for studying the late Cretaceous period. This site has yielded fossils of some of the most famous dinosaurs, including Tyrannosaurus rex, Triceratops, and Edmontosaurus. The fossils found in Hell Creek provide a detailed snapshot of the final days of the dinosaurs before the mass extinction event.

Fact 136: Dinosaur Coprolites Reveal Their Diet and Digestive Processes

Coprolites, or fossilized dinosaur dung, are a valuable source of information about dinosaur diets and digestive processes. By analyzing coprolites, paleontologists can identify the types of plants or animals that a dinosaur ate, as well as how their digestive system processed food. For example, coprolites from a T. rex have been found to contain crushed bone fragments, indicating that these predators could digest large amounts of bone.

Fact 137: Fossilized Pathologies Show Evidence of Dinosaur Injuries and Disease

Fossilized bones often show signs of injuries, disease, or other pathologies, providing insight into the challenges dinosaurs faced during their lives. For example, some dinosaur fossils show evidence of healed fractures, infections, or even tumors. These pathologies reveal that dinosaurs, like modern animals, were susceptible to injury and disease, and they also provide clues about how these animals might have coped with such conditions.

Fact 138: Amber Fossils Preserve Tiny Details of Dinosaur Era Life

Amber, fossilized tree resin, has preserved some of the most detailed and delicate fossils from the dinosaur era. Insects, plant material, and even feathers have been found trapped in amber, providing a unique window into the ecosystems that dinosaurs inhabited. One of the most remarkable discoveries in amber is a 99-million-year-old dinosaur tail with feathers, found in Myanmar, which offers unprecedented detail about the structure and appearance of dinosaur feathers.

Fact 139: The Dinosaur Renaissance Changed Our Understanding of Dinosaurs

The "Dinosaur Renaissance" refers to a period in the late 20th century when new discoveries and ideas dramatically changed our understanding of dinosaurs. This period saw the recognition that dinosaurs were more bird-like than reptilian, that they were likely warm-blooded, and that they were active, social animals rather than slow, solitary creatures. Key figures in this movement, such as John H. Ostrom and Robert T. Bakker, helped revolutionize the field of paleontology.

Fact 140: The Discovery of Oviraptor Nests Changed Perceptions

The discovery of Oviraptor nests in Mongolia in the 1920s initially led to the belief that these dinosaurs were egg thieves, preying on the eggs of other species. However, further study revealed that the nests actually belonged to Oviraptor itself, and that the dinosaur was likely caring for its own eggs. This discovery changed perceptions of Oviraptor from a villainous egg thief to a nurturing parent, highlighting the importance of careful interpretation in paleontology.

Fact 141: Fossilized Bonebeds Reveal Mass Death Events

Bonebeds, which are sites containing the remains of multiple individuals, provide evidence of mass death events that affected dinosaur populations. These events could have been caused by natural disasters such as floods, volcanic eruptions, or droughts. The study of bonebeds helps paleontologists understand the environmental conditions that led to these events and how they impacted dinosaur communities.

Fact 142: Dinosaur Tracks in the Paluxy River Stirred Controversy

The Paluxy River in Texas is famous for its fossilized dinosaur tracks, which include the footprints of both large sauropods and smaller theropods. In the 1930s, some claimed that these tracks also included human footprints, sparking controversy and debate. However, these "human" tracks have since been debunked as either misidentified dinosaur tracks or erosional features, reaffirming the importance of rigorous scientific analysis in paleontology.

Fact 143: The "Dueling Dinosaurs" Fossil Captures a Moment of Combat

The "Dueling Dinosaurs" fossil, discovered in Montana, captures a rare and dramatic moment in time—a fatal fight between a ceratopsian and a theropod, possibly a Triceratops and a Tyrannosaurus rex. This fossil, which shows both dinosaurs locked in combat, offers a unique glimpse into the behaviors and interactions of these ancient creatures. The specimen is still being studied and promises to provide valuable insights into the lives of these dinosaurs.

Fact 144: The Chicxulub Crater Provides Evidence of the Asteroid Impact

The Chicxulub crater, located on the Yucatan Peninsula in Mexico, is believed to be the impact site of the asteroid that caused the mass extinction of the dinosaurs 66 million years ago. The crater, which is over 110 miles wide, was discovered in the 1970s and has since been linked to the global layer of iridium-rich clay that marks the boundary between the Cretaceous and Paleogene periods. This discovery provides strong evidence for the impact hypothesis and its role in the extinction of the dinosaurs.

Fact 145: Fossilized Dinosaur Burrows Show Evidence of Shelter-Building

Fossilized burrows attributed to dinosaurs have been discovered in various locations, providing evidence that some species dug shelters for protection or nesting. These burrows, found in Australia and the United States, suggest that certain dinosaurs, particularly smaller species, used burrows to escape predators, extreme weather, or to raise their young. The discovery of these burrows adds another layer to our understanding of dinosaur behavior and adaptation.

Fact 146: The Yixian Formation is a Rich Source of Feathered Dinosaur Fossils

The Yixian Formation in northeastern China is one of the richest fossil sites for feathered dinosaurs. This early Cretaceous site has yielded an incredible array of fossils, including fully articulated skeletons of dinosaurs, birds, and other prehistoric creatures. The fossils from the Yixian Formation have provided critical evidence of the diversity of feathered dinosaurs and have helped to clarify the evolutionary relationship between dinosaurs and birds.

Fact 147: Fossils from the Morrison Formation Reveal a Dinosaur Ecosystem

The Morrison Formation, a sedimentary rock formation in the western United States, is one of the most significant sources of dinosaur fossils from the late Jurassic period. This formation has produced fossils of some of the most famous dinosaurs, including Allosaurus, Apatosaurus, and Stegosaurus. The Morrison Formation represents a diverse ecosystem, with evidence of various plant and animal species that lived alongside the dinosaurs.

Fact 148: Fossilized Teeth Offer Clues About Diet and Feeding Habits

Dinosaur teeth are some of the most common fossils found and can tell us a great deal about the diet and feeding habits of different species. For example, the sharp, serrated teeth of theropods like T. rex indicate a carnivorous diet, while the flat, grinding teeth of hadrosaurs suggest they were herbivores. Wear patterns on teeth can also reveal how dinosaurs processed their food, whether by chewing or swallowing it whole.

Fact 149: The "Ghost Ranch" Quarry is a Key Site for Early Dinosaur Fossils

The Ghost Ranch Quarry in New Mexico is a significant fossil site for studying the early evolution of dinosaurs. This site has produced numerous fossils of Coelophysis, one of the earliest known dinosaurs, dating back to the late Triassic period. The fossils from Ghost Ranch provide valuable insights into the anatomy and behavior of early dinosaurs, helping to fill in gaps in the evolutionary timeline.

Fact 150: Dinosaur Fossils Can Include Trace Fossils

Trace fossils, such as footprints, burrows, and coprolites, are indirect evidence of dinosaur activity and behavior. Unlike body fossils, which are the remains of the organism itself, trace fossils record the actions of dinosaurs, such as walking, feeding, or nesting. These fossils are crucial for understanding how dinosaurs interacted with their environment and provide a more complete picture of their daily lives.

Fact 151: The Burgess Shale Preserves Ancient Marine Life from the Cambrian Explosion

Although not a dinosaur fossil site, the Burgess Shale in Canada is one of the most important fossil sites in the world, preserving a diverse array of marine life from the Cambrian period, over 500 million years ago. The fossils from the Burgess Shale include some of the earliest known ancestors of dinosaurs, providing a glimpse into the distant origins of these ancient reptiles. The exceptional preservation of soft-bodied organisms in the Burgess Shale offers unique insights into the early evolution of life on Earth.

Fact 152: Dinosaur Fossils Provide Evidence of Climate and Environmental Changes

Dinosaur fossils can reveal much more than just the anatomy of these ancient creatures—they also provide clues about the climate and environment in which they lived. Isotopic analysis of dinosaur bones, teeth, and eggshells can indicate the temperature and humidity of the environment, while the types of plants found alongside dinosaur fossils can reveal details about the vegetation and ecosystems of the time. This information helps paleontologists reconstruct ancient climates and understand how dinosaurs adapted to changing conditions.

Fact 153: The Discovery of a Mummified Dinosaur Provided Exceptional Detail

In 2007, a remarkably well-preserved, mummified dinosaur was discovered in North Dakota. The fossil, known as "Dakota," is a hadrosaur with preserved skin and soft tissues, providing an unprecedented level of detail about its anatomy. The fossil reveals the texture of the dinosaur's skin, muscle placement, and even the contents of its stomach, offering a rare glimpse into the life of a dinosaur and how it looked in life.

Fact 154: The "Fighting Dinosaurs" Fossil Captures a Moment of Combat

One of the most famous dinosaur fossils ever discovered is the "Fighting Dinosaurs," found in Mongolia. This fossil captures a Velociraptor and a

Protoceratops locked in combat, with the Velociraptor's claw embedded in the Protoceratops' neck. This extraordinary fossil provides direct evidence of predatory behavior and offers a snapshot of a moment in time, frozen for millions of years.

Fact 155: The "Jurassic Mile" in Wyoming Yields Significant Fossils

The "Jurassic Mile" is a recently discovered fossil site in Wyoming that has yielded an incredible number of dinosaur fossils, including some species that are new to science. This site, which dates back to the Jurassic period, is providing paleontologists with a wealth of information about the diversity of life during this time and is expected to be a major source of new discoveries for years to come.

Fact 156: The Dreadnoughtus Fossil is One of the Most Complete Titanosaur Skeletons

Dreadnoughtus, discovered in Argentina in 2014, is one of the most complete skeletons of a titanosaur ever found. This massive dinosaur was over 85 feet long and weighed an estimated 65 tons. The completeness of the fossil has allowed scientists to study the anatomy of titanosaurs in unprecedented detail, providing new insights into how these giant dinosaurs lived and moved.

Fact 157: The Solnhofen Limestone is Famous for Preserving Archaeopteryx

The Solnhofen Limestone in Germany is one of the most famous fossil sites in the world, known for its exceptional preservation of Archaeopteryx, a transitional species between dinosaurs and birds. The fossils from Solnhofen include not only the bones of Archaeopteryx but also impressions of its feathers, providing crucial evidence for the evolution of flight in dinosaurs.

Fact 158: The "Death Pose" is Common in Dinosaur Fossils

Many dinosaur fossils are found in a characteristic "death pose," with the head thrown back and the tail arched over the body. This pose is believed to result from the contraction of muscles and tendons after death, particularly in waterlogged environments. The "death pose" provides clues about the conditions under which the dinosaur died and was fossilized, helping paleontologists understand the taphonomy, or process of fossilization.

Fact 159: The Ceratosaurus Fossil Was One of the First Dinosaurs Discovered in North America

Ceratosaurus, a large theropod dinosaur, was one of the first dinosaurs discovered in North America. The first fossil was found in Colorado in the late 19th century during the Bone Wars. This dinosaur is known for the distinctive horn on its nose and its large, serrated teeth, which suggest it was a formidable predator. The discovery of Ceratosaurus helped to establish North America as a major site for dinosaur fossils and spurred further exploration in the region.

Fact 160: Fossilized Dinosaur Skin Shows Patterns and Textures

In addition to bones, paleontologists have also discovered fossilized dinosaur skin, which provides insights into the patterns and textures of dinosaur integument. Some of these skin fossils show a scaly texture similar to that of modern reptiles, while others suggest the presence of more complex structures, possibly including proto-feathers. These discoveries have helped scientists to reconstruct the appearance of dinosaurs with greater accuracy.

Chapter 6: Theories of Dinosaur Extinction

The End of an Era: What Really Happened?

The extinction of the dinosaurs marks one of the most significant and dramatic events in Earth's history. Around 66 million years ago, nearly all dinosaur species vanished from the planet, bringing the Mesozoic Era to an abrupt end. While this mass extinction wiped out the non-avian dinosaurs, it paved the way for the rise of mammals and eventually, humans. In this chapter, we'll explore the various theories that scientists have proposed to explain the demise of these ancient giants.

Fact 161: The Asteroid Impact Hypothesis is the Leading Theory

The most widely accepted theory for the extinction of the dinosaurs is the asteroid impact hypothesis. This theory suggests that a massive asteroid, roughly 6 to 9 miles in diameter, struck the Earth near what is now the Yucatan Peninsula in Mexico. The impact created the Chicxulub crater, a structure over 110 miles wide, and released an enormous amount of energy, equivalent to billions of atomic bombs.

Fact 162: The Chicxulub Impact Caused Global Devastation

The asteroid impact at Chicxulub would have caused immediate and widespread devastation. The initial impact likely generated massive tsunamis, wildfires, and earthquakes. The energy released would have vaporized rock, sending it high into the atmosphere, where it rained down as molten debris, igniting fires across the planet. This would have led to a "nuclear winter" effect, blocking sunlight and drastically cooling the Earth's surface.

Fact 163: The Impact Winter Caused a Collapse in Photosynthesis

One of the most devastating consequences of the Chicxulub impact was the collapse of photosynthesis. The dust and aerosols thrown into the atmosphere would have blocked sunlight for months or even years, causing temperatures to plummet. Without sunlight, plants and phytoplankton—the base of the food chain—would have died off en masse, leading to a catastrophic collapse in ecosystems worldwide. This collapse would have affected herbivores first, and then the carnivores that depended on them.

Fact 164: The Deccan Traps Volcanism Also Played a Role

While the asteroid impact is the leading theory, some scientists believe that massive volcanic activity in the Deccan Traps, located in present-day India, also contributed to the extinction of the dinosaurs. The Deccan Traps are one of the largest volcanic features on Earth, and their eruptions spanned hundreds of thousands of years, releasing vast amounts of volcanic gases like sulfur dioxide and carbon dioxide into the atmosphere.

Fact 165: Volcanic Eruptions Could Have Caused Acid Rain

The volcanic eruptions in the Deccan Traps would have released significant amounts of sulfur dioxide, which could have combined with water vapor in the atmosphere to create sulfuric acid. This would have led to acid rain, which could have devastated plant life and disrupted freshwater ecosystems. The acidification of oceans and lakes would have had severe impacts on marine life, further destabilizing the food chain.

Fact 166: The Combination of Volcanism and Impact Created a Double Whammy

Some scientists propose that the combination of the Chicxulub impact and the Deccan Traps volcanism created a "double whammy" that led to the mass extinction. The impact would have caused immediate and widespread devastation, while the prolonged volcanic activity exacerbated the environmental changes, leading to a gradual but sustained collapse of ecosystems. This theory suggests that the two events were not mutually exclusive but rather worked together to bring about the extinction.

Fact 167: Climate Change Was a Factor in the Extinction

Even before the asteroid impact and volcanic eruptions, the Earth was undergoing significant climate changes during the late Cretaceous period. Evidence suggests that global temperatures were already fluctuating, and sea levels were rising and falling, leading to habitat loss for many species. These environmental stresses could have weakened dinosaur populations, making them more vulnerable to the catastrophic events that followed.

Fact 168: The Food Chain Collapse Was Devastating

The extinction of the dinosaurs was likely driven by a collapse in the food chain. As photosynthesis ceased due to the lack of sunlight, plants and phytoplankton died off, causing herbivorous dinosaurs to starve. With their food sources gone, carnivorous dinosaurs would have followed suit. The collapse of the food chain would have been swift and devastating, leading to the extinction of nearly all dinosaur species.

Fact 169: Marine Reptiles and Pterosaurs Also Went Extinct

The mass extinction at the end of the Cretaceous didn't just affect the dinosaurs on land. Marine reptiles, like the mosasaurs and plesiosaurs, and flying reptiles, like the pterosaurs, also went extinct. The loss of marine phytoplankton due to the impact winter would have led to the collapse of marine food chains, while the drastic climate changes would have affected the habitats of pterosaurs, leading to their extinction as well.

Fact 170: Small Mammals Survived and Thrived After the Extinction

While the mass extinction wiped out the dinosaurs, it created opportunities for small mammals to thrive. These mammals were small, burrowing creatures that could have survived the extreme conditions by hiding underground and feeding on detritus or insects. With the extinction of the dinosaurs, mammals rapidly diversified and evolved, eventually leading to the rise of the mammals that dominate the Earth today, including humans.

Fact 171: Birds Are the Last Surviving Dinosaurs

While most dinosaurs went extinct, one group survived: the birds. Birds are the direct descendants of small, feathered theropods, and their survival is one of the most fascinating aspects of the extinction event. Birds were likely able to survive because of their small size, ability to fly, and varied diets, which may have included seeds, insects, and other resources that were more abundant after the extinction event.

Fact 172: The K-T Boundary Marks the Moment of Extinction

The K-T boundary (now more accurately called the K-Pg boundary) is a distinct layer of sediment found all over the world that marks the moment of the dinosaur extinction. This layer, rich in iridium—a metal rare on Earth but common in asteroids—provides strong evidence for the asteroid impact hypothesis. The K-T boundary serves as a stark geological marker of one of the most significant events in Earth's history.

Fact 173: The Extinction Was Likely a Gradual Process

While the asteroid impact was a sudden and catastrophic event, the extinction of the dinosaurs was likely a more gradual process. Some species may have survived for thousands of years after the impact, gradually succumbing to the harsh conditions and lack of resources. The extinction was a complex event with multiple factors contributing over time, rather than a single, instantaneous die-off.

Fact 174: Some Dinosaurs Were Already in Decline Before the Impact

There is evidence to suggest that some dinosaur species were already in decline before the asteroid impact. Fossil records show a decrease in diversity and abundance in certain groups of dinosaurs during the late Cretaceous, possibly due to climate change, habitat loss, or other environmental factors. This decline may have made dinosaurs more vulnerable to the catastrophic events that followed.

Fact 175: The Impact Hypothesis Was Proposed in 1980

The asteroid impact hypothesis was first proposed in 1980 by a team of scientists led by Luis Alvarez and his son Walter Alvarez. They discovered a layer of iridium-rich clay at the K-T boundary, which they suggested was evidence of an asteroid impact. Their hypothesis revolutionized our understanding of the dinosaur extinction and sparked decades of research into the causes of this mass extinction event.

Fact 176: The "Dinosaur Pompeii" Preserves a Moment in Time

In 2011, paleontologists discovered an extraordinary fossil site in North Dakota, known as the Tanis site, which preserves the immediate aftermath of the Chicxulub impact. Dubbed the "Dinosaur Pompeii," this site contains fossilized fish, plants, and other organisms that were killed by the impact's effects, including the initial shockwaves and subsequent tsunamis. The site provides a rare and detailed snapshot of the extinction event as it happened.

Fact 177: The Extinction Was a Global Event

The extinction of the dinosaurs was a global event, affecting ecosystems all over the world. Fossil evidence shows that species from every continent were affected, from the dinosaurs of North America to the marine reptiles of Europe and the pterosaurs of South America. The widespread nature of the extinction suggests that the causes—whether asteroid impact, volcanic activity, or climate change—had planet-wide effects.

Fact 178: The Extinction Opened Up Ecological Niches

The mass extinction at the end of the Cretaceous opened up ecological niches that had been dominated by dinosaurs for over 150 million years. With the dinosaurs gone, other groups of animals, particularly mammals, were able to evolve and diversify to fill these niches. This led to the rapid evolution of new species and the eventual rise of mammals as the dominant land animals.

Fact 179: The Extinction Was the Fifth Major Mass Extinction Event

The extinction of the dinosaurs was the fifth major mass extinction event in Earth's history. Previous mass extinctions, such as the Permian-Triassic extinction, had also caused significant losses in biodiversity. However, the

Cretaceous-Paleogene extinction is perhaps the most famous due to its role in ending the age of the dinosaurs and reshaping life on Earth.

Fact 180: Research on Dinosaur Extinction Continues to Evolve

Our understanding of dinosaur extinction is still evolving as new discoveries and technologies emerge. Ongoing research continues to refine our knowledge of the events leading up to the extinction, the impact of the Chicxulub asteroid, and the role of volcanic activity in the Deccan Traps. As scientists uncover new evidence, the story of how the dinosaurs went extinct—and how life on Earth recovered—becomes ever more complex and fascinating.

Fact 181: The Chicxulub Impact May Have Triggered a Mega-Tsunami

The Chicxulub impact likely triggered a massive tsunami, possibly one of the largest in Earth's history. The force of the impact would have displaced vast amounts of water, creating waves that could have traveled thousands of miles. Evidence of this mega-tsunami has been found in geological formations around the world, including deposits of tsunami-generated sediments far inland from ancient coastlines.

Fact 182: Microtektites Found in Fossil Sites Support the Impact Hypothesis

Microtektites, tiny glassy particles formed by the intense heat of an asteroid impact, have been found in various fossil sites around the world, dating to the K-Pg boundary. These particles are another piece of evidence supporting the impact hypothesis. They were likely ejected into the atmosphere by the Chicxulub impact and then rained down over vast areas, providing a timeline marker for the event.

Fact 183: The Extinction Event Helped Shape Modern Biodiversity

The mass extinction that wiped out the dinosaurs also paved the way for the evolution of many of the species we see today. With the dominant dinosaurs gone, mammals, birds, and other surviving species diversified rapidly, leading to the rich biodiversity of the modern world. The extinction event acted as a reset button, allowing new forms of life to emerge and thrive.

Fact 184: The Eventual Discovery of the Chicxulub Crater Solved a Major Mystery

The discovery of the Chicxulub crater in the late 1970s and early 1980s was a turning point in understanding the dinosaur extinction. Prior to this discovery, the cause of the mass extinction was a topic of much speculation, with various theories proposed, including volcanic activity, climate change, and disease. The identification of the crater provided the physical evidence needed to support the asteroid impact hypothesis.

Fact 185: The Impact Would Have Caused Severe Acidification of the Oceans

In addition to blocking sunlight, the asteroid impact likely caused the oceans to become more acidic. The sulfur dioxide and other gases released by the impact would have mixed with water vapor in the atmosphere, leading to acid rain and acidification of the oceans. This would have had devastating effects on marine life, particularly for organisms with calcium carbonate shells, such as ammonites, which went extinct during this event.

Fact 186: The Cretaceous-Paleogene Extinction was Selective

While the Cretaceous-Paleogene extinction was catastrophic, it was also selective. Not all life forms were equally affected—while most non-avian dinosaurs, large marine reptiles, and many plants and invertebrates went extinct, other groups, such as mammals, birds, and crocodiles, survived. This selectivity likely depended on a variety of factors, including size, habitat, and diet.

Fact 187: The Extinction Led to the Evolution of Large Mammals

After the extinction of the dinosaurs, mammals began to rapidly evolve and diversify. Freed from competition with dinosaurs, mammals adapted to fill the ecological niches left vacant by the extinction. Over time, some mammals evolved into larger forms, leading to the rise of megafauna such as mammoths, mastodons, and giant ground sloths, which dominated the landscape during the subsequent epochs.

Fact 188: The Extinction May Have Led to the Development of New Plant Species

The extinction event had a significant impact on plant life as well. The loss of sunlight and the subsequent cooling of the planet would have devastated many plant species. However, this also created opportunities for new plants to evolve and thrive. The post-extinction period saw the rise of flowering plants (angiosperms), which diversified and spread rapidly, leading to the dominance of angiosperms in the modern world.

Fact 189: Some Scientists Believe Multiple Impacts Contributed to the Extinction

While the Chicxulub impact is the most well-known, some scientists believe that other asteroid impacts may have occurred around the same time and contributed to the extinction. Evidence of smaller impact craters from the same period has been found in other parts of the world. These additional impacts may have compounded the environmental stress caused by the Chicxulub event, leading to the widespread extinction of species.

Fact 190: The Extinction Event Led to a Restructuring of Earth's Ecosystems

The extinction of the dinosaurs and other species at the end of the Cretaceous led to a major restructuring of Earth's ecosystems. With many dominant species gone, new ecosystems emerged, characterized by different species of plants and animals. This restructuring laid the foundation for the modern ecosystems we see today, with mammals, birds, and flowering plants becoming the dominant forms of life.

Chapter 7: Dinosaurs in Modern Science

From Bones to DNA: The Cutting Edge of Paleontology

The study of dinosaurs has come a long way since the first fossil discoveries in the 19th century. Today, modern science continues to revolutionize our understanding of these ancient creatures. Advances in technology, new fossil discoveries, and groundbreaking research have all contributed to a more detailed and accurate picture of what dinosaurs were like, how they lived, and how they evolved. In this chapter, we'll explore the ways in which modern science is unlocking the secrets of the dinosaurs.

Fact 191: CT Scanning Allows Scientists to Study Fossils in Detail

Computed tomography (CT) scanning has become an essential tool in paleontology, allowing scientists to study the internal structure of fossils without damaging them. By taking a series of X-ray images from different angles, CT scans create a detailed 3D model of a fossil, revealing intricate details such as bone structure, brain cavities, and even the presence of soft tissues. This technology has revolutionized the way scientists examine and understand dinosaur anatomy.

Fact 192: Isotope Analysis Provides Clues About Dinosaur Diets

Isotope analysis is a technique used to study the chemical composition of dinosaur bones, teeth, and eggshells. By examining the ratios of certain isotopes, such as carbon and oxygen, scientists can infer details about a dinosaur's diet, migration patterns, and the environments they lived in. For example, the study of oxygen isotopes in dinosaur teeth can reveal whether a dinosaur drank freshwater or seawater, providing insights into its habitat.

Fact 193: Dinosaur Feathers Were Analyzed for Color Using Fossil Pigments

One of the most exciting developments in paleontology has been the discovery of fossilized pigments in dinosaur feathers. These pigments, known as melanosomes, have allowed scientists to determine the colors and patterns of some dinosaurs for the first time. For example, the small theropod Sinosauropteryx was found to have had a striped tail and a reddish-brown color. This analysis has provided a more accurate depiction of what dinosaurs may have looked like in life.

Fact 194: Fossil DNA Could Offer New Insights into Dinosaur Genetics

While the extraction of complete dinosaur DNA remains a distant possibility, scientists have successfully retrieved fragments of genetic material from ancient organisms, such as Neanderthals and mammoths. In 2020, researchers identified proteins in a 195-million-year-old Lufengosaurus fossil, the oldest proteins ever discovered. Although full dinosaur DNA recovery may be out of reach, studying these ancient proteins could offer valuable insights into dinosaur genetics and evolution.

Fact 195: The Study of Growth Rings Reveals Dinosaur Lifespan and Growth Rates

Just like trees, dinosaur bones have growth rings that can be analyzed to determine their age and growth rates. By counting these rings and examining their thickness, scientists can estimate how fast a dinosaur grew and how long it lived. This technique has revealed that some dinosaurs, like the giant sauropods, grew incredibly quickly, reaching their massive sizes in just a few decades.

Fact 196: The Use of Biomechanics Helps Understand Dinosaur Movement

Biomechanics, the study of the mechanical aspects of living organisms, has become a key area of research in paleontology. By creating computer models of dinosaur skeletons and simulating their movement, scientists can explore how these animals walked, ran, and even flew. These models have provided insights into the locomotion of dinosaurs, such as how Tyrannosaurus rex balanced its massive head and tail while running, or how the pterosaur Quetzalcoatlus achieved flight.

Fact 197: Bone Histology Offers Clues About Dinosaur Physiology

Bone histology, the microscopic study of bone tissue, allows scientists to explore the physiology of dinosaurs in detail. By examining thin sections of fossilized bone under a microscope, researchers can identify the types of cells present and the rate at which the bone was growing. This information helps scientists understand whether dinosaurs were warm-blooded or cold-blooded, how they grew, and how they healed from injuries.

Fact 198: Fossilized Soft Tissues Provide Unprecedented Insights

The discovery of fossilized soft tissues, such as skin, muscles, and even blood vessels, has provided paleontologists with unprecedented insights into dinosaur biology. For example, in 2005, a team of scientists led by Mary Schweitzer discovered flexible blood vessels and cells within a Tyrannosaurus rex femur. These rare finds have sparked debates about the preservation of soft tissues and their potential for further study.

Fact 199: Paleontologists Use Virtual Reality to Reconstruct Dinosaurs

Virtual reality (VR) is being used to create immersive, 3D reconstructions of dinosaurs and their environments. By combining fossil data with advanced computer graphics, scientists can build detailed models of dinosaurs and place them in virtual ecosystems. These reconstructions allow paleontologists to explore how dinosaurs interacted with their environment and each other, offering new perspectives on their behavior and ecology.

Fact 200: The Study of Dinosaur Eggs Reveals Reproductive Strategies

Fossilized dinosaur eggs provide important clues about dinosaur reproduction. By studying the size, shape, and composition of these eggs, scientists can infer details about the nesting behavior, incubation methods, and developmental stages of dinosaur embryos. For example, some eggs show evidence of hard shells, similar to those of modern birds, suggesting that these dinosaurs laid their eggs in open nests and relied on environmental conditions to incubate them.

Fact 201: Fossil Footprints Reveal Social Behavior

Fossilized footprints, or ichnites, offer a unique window into the behavior of dinosaurs. By analyzing trackways, scientists can determine the speed, gait, and social behavior of dinosaurs. For example, parallel trackways of sauropods suggest they moved in herds, while the tracks of theropods sometimes show evidence of pack hunting. These footprints provide direct evidence of how dinosaurs moved and interacted with each other.

Fact 202: Paleontologists Are Using Lasers to Study Fossils

Laser-stimulated fluorescence (LSF) is a technique that uses lasers to reveal hidden details in fossils. When a fossil is illuminated with a laser, certain minerals within the fossil fluoresce, highlighting features that are not visible under normal light. This technique has been used to discover details such as the presence of soft tissues, skin patterns, and even the arrangement of muscles in fossils.

Fact 203: The Evolutionary Link Between Dinosaurs and Birds is Strengthened by Modern Research

Modern research continues to strengthen the evolutionary link between dinosaurs and birds. Fossils of feathered dinosaurs, such as Archaeopteryx and Microraptor, show clear similarities to modern birds, including the structure of their feathers, bones, and respiratory systems. Genetic studies of birds have also provided evidence of shared ancestry with theropod dinosaurs, confirming that birds are the direct descendants of these ancient reptiles.

Fact 204: The Discovery of New Dinosaur Species Continues at a Rapid Pace

Despite being extinct for 66 million years, new species of dinosaurs are still being discovered at an astonishing rate. On average, paleontologists describe about 50 new dinosaur species each year, thanks to ongoing fossil discoveries around the world. These new finds are expanding our understanding of the diversity of dinosaurs and revealing new insights into their evolution, behavior, and ecology.

Fact 205: Paleogenomics Could Unlock Dinosaur Genomes

Paleogenomics, the study of ancient DNA and genomes, is an emerging field that holds the potential to unlock the genetic secrets of dinosaurs. Although recovering intact dinosaur DNA is currently beyond our reach, the study of ancient DNA in other extinct species, such as mammoths and Neanderthals, is providing valuable techniques and insights that could one day be applied to dinosaurs. This research could offer a deeper understanding of dinosaur biology, evolution, and even the possibility of de-extinction.

Fact 206: Scientists Use Synchrotron Imaging to Analyze Fossils

Synchrotron imaging is a powerful technique that uses high-energy X-rays to analyze fossils in incredible detail. This method allows scientists to see the internal structure of fossils at the microscopic level, revealing features such as blood vessels, bone growth patterns, and even the presence of minerals that indicate the color of feathers or skin. Synchrotron imaging is helping paleontologists to study fossils in ways that were previously impossible.

Fact 207: Advances in Cladistics Have Refined Dinosaur Classification

Cladistics, a method of classifying organisms based on common ancestry, has revolutionized the way scientists understand the relationships between different dinosaur species. By analyzing shared characteristics and constructing evolutionary trees, or cladograms, paleontologists can trace the evolutionary history of dinosaurs and identify the traits that link them to other groups, such as birds. This approach has led to a more accurate and detailed classification of dinosaurs.

Fact 208: The Use of Machine Learning is Revolutionizing Paleontology

Machine learning and artificial intelligence (AI) are increasingly being used in paleontology to analyze vast amounts of fossil data. These technologies can identify patterns and make predictions that would be difficult or impossible for humans to detect. For example, AI algorithms can be used to classify fossils, reconstruct dinosaur skeletons, and even predict where new fossils might be found based on geological data.

Fact 209: The Study of Dinosaur Pathologies Provides Insights into Their Health

The study of pathologies, or diseases, in dinosaur fossils has provided insights into the health and biology of these ancient creatures. Fossilized bones often show signs of injuries, infections, and other conditions, such as arthritis or cancer. By analyzing these pathologies, scientists can learn about the challenges dinosaurs faced during their lives and how they might have adapted to cope with injuries or illnesses.

Fact 210: Geochemical Analysis Reveals Dinosaur Diets and Environments

Geochemical analysis involves studying the chemical composition of fossils and the surrounding rocks to gain insights into dinosaur diets and environments. By analyzing isotopes, trace elements, and organic molecules, scientists can determine what dinosaurs ate, where they lived, and how they interacted with their environment. This technique has been used to study everything from the diet of herbivorous dinosaurs to the environmental conditions of the late Cretaceous.

Fact 211: The Study of Dinosaur Microbiomes is an Emerging Field

The microbiome, the collection of microorganisms that live in and on an organism, plays a crucial role in health and digestion. Although we can't directly study the microbiomes of dinosaurs, scientists are beginning to explore this field by analyzing the gut contents of fossilized remains and comparing them to the microbiomes of modern animals. This research could provide insights into the diets, health, and evolution of dinosaurs.

Fact 212: The "Bristol Dinosaur Project" Uses Digital Tools to Reconstruct Dinosaurs

The "Bristol Dinosaur Project" is an initiative that uses digital tools to reconstruct the skeletons and muscles of dinosaurs in 3D. By combining fossil data with computer simulations, researchers can create accurate models of how dinosaurs moved, hunted, and interacted with their environment. These digital reconstructions provide a dynamic view of dinosaur biology and offer new insights into their behavior and ecology.

Fact 213: Paleontologists Are Studying Dinosaur Eggs to Understand Development

Dinosaur eggs offer a unique window into the development of these ancient creatures. By studying the size, shape, and structure of fossilized eggs, as well as the embryos preserved within them, scientists can learn about the growth and development of dinosaurs before they hatched. This research has revealed that some dinosaurs, like modern birds, developed rapidly in the egg, while others had longer incubation periods.

Fact 214: Dinosaur "Mummies" Preserve Exceptional Detail

Fossilized dinosaur "mummies," where skin, muscles, and other soft tissues are preserved alongside the bones, offer an exceptional level of detail about dinosaur anatomy. These rare fossils, such as the famous "Leonardo" Brachylophosaurus, provide a wealth of information about the appearance, muscle structure, and even the digestive systems of dinosaurs. The study of these mummies is helping paleontologists to create more accurate reconstructions of how dinosaurs looked and lived.

Fact 215: The "Jehol Biota" Provides Insights into Early Cretaceous Ecosystems

The Jehol Biota, a fossil assemblage from northeastern China, has provided some of the most detailed insights into early Cretaceous ecosystems. This site has yielded an incredible array of well-preserved fossils, including feathered dinosaurs, early birds, and mammals. The Jehol Biota has helped scientists to understand the diversity of life during this period and the evolutionary relationships between different groups of organisms.

Fact 216: "Virtual Fossils" Allow Scientists to Study Rare Specimens

Virtual fossils, created through high-resolution scanning and 3D modeling, allow scientists to study rare and fragile fossils without the risk of damaging them. These digital models can be shared with researchers around the world, enabling collaborative studies and new discoveries. Virtual fossils are also used in education, allowing students to explore and interact with fossils in ways that were previously impossible.

Fact 217: The "Dinosaur Renaissance" Continues to Influence Modern Research

The "Dinosaur Renaissance," a period of renewed interest and discovery in the study of dinosaurs during the late 20th century, continues to influence modern research. The ideas and discoveries that emerged during this time, such as the recognition that dinosaurs were more bird-like than reptilian, have shaped our current understanding of dinosaur biology and evolution. The ongoing influence of this period is evident in the continued emphasis on studying dinosaurs as dynamic, active creatures.

Fact 218: The Study of Dinosaur Tracks Offers Clues About Social Behavior

Dinosaur tracks are more than just footprints—they offer valuable clues about the social behavior of dinosaurs. By analyzing trackways, scientists can determine whether dinosaurs traveled in groups, how they moved, and even how they interacted with each other. For example, parallel trackways suggest that some dinosaurs, like sauropods, traveled in herds, while overlapping tracks might indicate that theropods hunted in packs.

Fact 219: Paleontologists Use X-Rays to Examine Fossils

X-rays are commonly used in paleontology to examine fossils without damaging them. This technique allows scientists to see inside fossils, revealing hidden details such as the structure of bones, teeth, and even soft tissues. X-rays have been particularly useful in studying fossilized embryos, helping scientists to understand the development of dinosaurs from egg to adult.

Fact 220: The Discovery of "Nanotyrannus" Sparked Debate

The discovery of "Nanotyrannus," a small, agile theropod, sparked a debate among paleontologists about whether it represents a distinct species or simply a juvenile Tyrannosaurus rex. Some scientists argue that Nanotyrannus is a separate species, while others believe it is a young T. rex that has not yet reached its full size. This debate highlights the challenges of interpreting the fossil record and the importance of continued research.

Fact 221: The "Paleocene Dinosaurs" Hypothesis Suggests Some Dinosaurs Survived the Extinction

The "Paleocene Dinosaurs" hypothesis suggests that some dinosaurs may have survived the mass extinction event at the end of the Cretaceous and lived into the early Paleocene epoch. This controversial idea is based on the discovery of dinosaur fossils in Paleocene-aged rocks, although most paleontologists believe these fossils were re-deposited from older layers. If proven true, this hypothesis would challenge our understanding of the timing and extent of the dinosaur extinction.

Fact 222: The "Archaeoraptor" Scandal Highlighted the Importance of Scientific Rigor

The "Archaeoraptor" scandal in the late 1990s highlighted the importance of scientific rigor and skepticism in paleontology. Originally hailed as a missing link between dinosaurs and birds, the fossil was later revealed to be a forgery, made by combining parts of different fossils. This incident underscored the need for careful examination and verification of fossil discoveries, especially those that make extraordinary claims.

Fact 223: Dinosaur Fossils Provide Insights into Ancient Climate Change

Dinosaur fossils are valuable tools for studying ancient climate change. By analyzing the isotopic composition of dinosaur bones, teeth, and eggshells, scientists can reconstruct past climates and understand how dinosaurs adapted to changing environments. This research has revealed that dinosaurs lived in a wide range of climates, from tropical forests to polar regions, and that they were remarkably adaptable to different environmental conditions.

Fact 224: The Use of Genetic Engineering Could One Day Resurrect Dinosaurs

The idea of resurrecting dinosaurs through genetic engineering, popularized by the "Jurassic Park" franchise, remains speculative but not entirely outside the realm of possibility. Advances in cloning, gene editing, and synthetic biology have raised the prospect of "de-extinction," where scientists might one day recreate extinct species by reconstructing their genomes. While ethical and technical challenges remain, the study of ancient DNA continues to push the boundaries of what is possible in genetics.

Fact 225: Dinosaurs in Modern Science Represent a Fascinating Intersection of History and Technology

The study of dinosaurs is a dynamic field that combines elements of history, biology, geology, and cutting-edge technology. As scientists continue to develop new tools and techniques, our understanding of these ancient creatures becomes ever more detailed and accurate. From the discovery of new species to the analysis of ancient DNA, dinosaurs remain at the forefront of scientific research, offering endless opportunities for discovery and exploration.

Chapter 8: Dinosaurs in Popular Culture

From the Silver Screen to the Toy Aisle: Dinosaurs Today

Dinosaurs have captured the human imagination like few other creatures. From blockbuster movies and television shows to toys, books, and video games, these ancient reptiles have become an enduring part of popular culture. Their enormous size, fearsome appearance, and mysterious extinction make them fascinating subjects for storytelling, art, and education. In this chapter, we'll explore how dinosaurs have influenced popular culture and how they continue to shape our perceptions of the prehistoric world.

Fact 226: "Jurassic Park" Revolutionized the Way We See Dinosaurs

When "Jurassic Park" premiered in 1993, it set a new standard for how dinosaurs were portrayed in film. Directed by Steven Spielberg and based on the novel by Michael Crichton, the movie combined cutting-edge special effects with gripping storytelling to bring dinosaurs to life in a way never seen before. The film's realistic depictions of dinosaurs, particularly the terrifying Velociraptors and the mighty Tyrannosaurus rex, captivated audiences and sparked renewed interest in paleontology.

Fact 227: "The Land Before Time" Introduced Dinosaurs to a New Generation

Released in 1988, "The Land Before Time" is an animated film that introduced dinosaurs to a new generation of children. The movie follows the adventures of Littlefoot, a young Apatosaurus, and his friends as they journey to find the Great Valley, a safe haven from predators and natural disasters. The film's success led to a long-running franchise, including sequels, television series, and merchandise, making dinosaurs a beloved part of childhood for millions.

Fact 228: Dinosaurs Are a Staple of Science Fiction Literature

Dinosaurs have long been a favorite subject in science fiction literature. Early examples include Arthur Conan Doyle's 1912 novel "The Lost World," in which a group of explorers discovers a plateau in South America where dinosaurs still live. This theme of "lost worlds" where dinosaurs survive has been explored in countless books and films, reflecting humanity's fascination with the possibility of encountering these ancient creatures in modern times.

Fact 229: Dinosaur Toys Have Been Popular for Over a Century

Dinosaur toys have been popular with children for over a century, providing a hands-on way to explore the prehistoric world. From the simple plastic figurines of the mid-20th century to today's highly detailed and scientifically accurate models, dinosaur toys have evolved alongside our understanding of these creatures. Iconic brands like LEGO and Mattel have released numerous dinosaur-themed sets, further cementing their place in the toy industry.

Fact 230: "Godzilla" Turned Dinosaurs Into Cultural Icons

First appearing in the 1954 Japanese film "Gojira," Godzilla is a giant, dinosaur-like monster that has become a cultural icon in its own right. Created as a metaphor for the dangers of nuclear weapons, Godzilla has appeared in dozens of films, television shows, and comic books, often depicted as both a destructive force and a protector of humanity. Godzilla's design, inspired by various prehistoric reptiles, has made it one of the most recognizable "dinosaurs" in popular culture.

Fact 231: Dinosaurs Are a Popular Theme in Video Games

Dinosaurs have been a popular theme in video games for decades. From early arcade games like "Dino Crisis" to modern titles like "ARK: Survival Evolved," where players can tame and ride dinosaurs, these ancient creatures offer endless possibilities for interactive entertainment. Video games allow players to explore prehistoric worlds, battle fearsome predators, and even manage their own dinosaur parks, combining education with excitement.

Fact 232: Dinosaur Museums Attract Millions of Visitors Each Year

Museums dedicated to dinosaurs attract millions of visitors each year, offering a chance to see real fossils and life-sized reconstructions up close. Institutions like the American Museum of Natural History in New York, the Natural History Museum in London, and the Field Museum in Chicago are home to some of the most famous dinosaur exhibits in the world. These museums play a crucial role in educating the public about paleontology and keeping the fascination with dinosaurs alive.

Fact 233: Dinosaurs Are a Popular Subject in Art and Illustration

Dinosaurs have inspired countless artists and illustrators, from early scientific illustrations to modern digital art. Paleoart, the artistic reconstruction of prehistoric life, plays an important role in shaping our understanding of dinosaurs. Artists like Charles R. Knight, Zdeněk Burian, and modern paleoartists like Gregory S. Paul and Luis Rey have brought dinosaurs to life in vivid detail, influencing how these creatures are depicted in books, films, and museums.

Fact 234: Dinosaur Documentaries Bring Prehistory to Life

Documentaries about dinosaurs have brought the prehistoric world into living rooms around the globe. One of the most influential dinosaur documentaries is the BBC's "Walking with Dinosaurs," which aired in 1999. Using cutting-edge CGI and animatronics, the series depicted the lives of dinosaurs as never seen before, setting a new standard for paleontological documentaries. Since then, numerous documentaries have explored the latest discoveries and theories about dinosaur life.

Fact 235: Dinosaurs Are a Common Motif in Fashion and Design

Dinosaurs have made their way into fashion and design, appearing on everything from T-shirts and jewelry to home décor. The image of the dinosaur has become a symbol of strength, mystery, and the distant past, making it a popular motif for both children's and adult's clothing. Designers often play with the iconic shapes of dinosaurs, creating stylized or humorous interpretations that appeal to a wide audience.

Fact 236: Dinosaur Comics Blend Humor with Science

Dinosaurs have found a unique place in the world of webcomics, where artists blend humor with scientific facts. One popular example is "Dinosaur Comics" by Ryan North, which features the same six-panel layout for every strip, with dialogue-driven humor that often touches on philosophy, science, and the absurdities of life. These comics use dinosaurs as characters to explore a wide range of topics, making science approachable and entertaining.

Fact 237: Dinosaurs Have Influenced Theme Park Attractions

Dinosaurs are a major attraction in theme parks around the world. The most famous example is "Jurassic Park: The Ride," originally opened at Universal

Studios in 1996. This ride, based on the popular film franchise, immerses visitors in a world where dinosaurs have been brought back to life. Other parks, such as Dinoland USA at Disney's Animal Kingdom, offer interactive experiences and educational exhibits, blending entertainment with a love for paleontology.

Fact 238: The "Dinosaur Renaissance" Influenced Pop Culture

The "Dinosaur Renaissance," a period of renewed interest in dinosaurs during the late 20th century, significantly influenced how these creatures are portrayed in popular culture. This era saw a shift from depicting dinosaurs as slow, lumbering reptiles to dynamic, active animals more closely related to birds. This change in scientific perspective was reflected in movies, television shows, and books, leading to more accurate and exciting portrayals of dinosaurs.

Fact 239: Dinosaurs Have Appeared on Currency and Stamps

Dinosaurs have even made their way onto currency and postage stamps. Several countries have issued coins and stamps featuring dinosaurs, celebrating their national heritage or significant fossil discoveries. These collectibles are popular among both numismatists and paleontology enthusiasts, offering a unique way to commemorate these ancient creatures.

Fact 240: Dinosaur-Themed Books Span All Ages and Genres

Books about dinosaurs are popular across all ages and genres, from children's picture books to scientific treatises. Classics like "Danny and the Dinosaur" and "Dinotopia" have introduced young readers to the wonders of the prehistoric world, while more scholarly works like "The Dinosaur Heresies" by Robert T. Bakker have challenged conventional thinking about dinosaur biology and evolution. The enduring popularity of dinosaur-themed books reflects our ongoing fascination with these creatures.

Fact 241: Dinosaurs Are a Popular Subject in Music

Dinosaurs have also made their way into the world of music. Songs like "Walk the Dinosaur" by Was (Not Was) and "Dinosaur" by Kesha have used dinosaurs as metaphors for fun, power, or even outdated ideas. Additionally, bands like T. Rex, named after the famous dinosaur, have cemented the connection between prehistoric creatures and rock music, using the imagery of dinosaurs to convey a sense of raw energy and rebellion.

Fact 242: Dinosaurs Have Been Used in Advertising

Dinosaurs have long been a popular choice in advertising, used to grab attention and evoke a sense of awe and wonder. From breakfast cereals to automobiles, dinosaurs are often used to symbolize strength, durability, and timelessness. Their iconic status in popular culture makes them an effective tool for marketers looking to create memorable and impactful campaigns.

Fact 243: Dinosaur Skeletons Have Become Popular Public Art Displays

Life-sized replicas of dinosaur skeletons have become popular public art displays, often appearing in unexpected places like city squares, airports, and shopping centers. These displays bring a sense of wonder and history to public spaces, allowing people to experience the scale and majesty of dinosaurs outside of traditional museum settings. They also serve as a reminder of the ancient past that still captures our imagination today.

Fact 244: Dinosaurs in Mythology and Folklore

Even before the scientific study of dinosaurs began, large fossils found by ancient civilizations may have inspired myths and legends about giants and dragons. In China, "dragon bones" were collected and used in traditional medicine, while in

Europe, some scholars believe that dinosaur fossils may have contributed to tales of dragons. These ancient creatures, though long extinct, continue to influence our mythology and storytelling traditions.

Fact 245: Dinosaurs Are a Symbol of Endurance and Adaptation

In popular culture, dinosaurs often symbolize endurance, adaptation, and the passage of time. Despite their extinction, dinosaurs are seen as a testament to the power and diversity of life on Earth. They remind us of the transient nature of existence and the need to adapt to changing environments. This symbolism is often used in literature, art, and media to convey themes of survival and resilience.

Fact 246: Dinosaur Exhibitions Travel the World

Traveling dinosaur exhibitions bring the wonders of paleontology to audiences around the globe. These exhibitions feature life-sized models, fossil replicas, and interactive displays that educate and entertain visitors of all ages. Popular exhibitions like "Jurassic World: The Exhibition" and "Dinosaurs in Motion" tour cities worldwide, making the prehistoric world accessible to people who may not have the opportunity to visit major natural history museums.

Fact 247: Dinosaurs Continue to Inspire New Discoveries

Dinosaurs remain a powerful source of inspiration for scientists, artists, and storytellers alike. Each new fossil discovery adds to our understanding of these ancient creatures, sparking the imagination and leading to new interpretations in popular culture. The fascination with dinosaurs shows no signs of fading, as they continue to capture our hearts and minds, reminding us of a world long gone but never forgotten.

Fact 248: Dinosaurs Are a Common Theme in Educational Content

Educational content about dinosaurs is widely popular, ranging from children's programming to documentaries for adults. Shows like "Dinosaur Train" introduce young viewers to different species and paleontological concepts, while documentaries like "Planet Dinosaur" provide in-depth explorations of the latest scientific findings. Dinosaurs serve as an engaging way to teach concepts in biology, geology, and evolutionary theory.

Fact 249: Dinosaurs in Comic Books and Graphic Novels

Dinosaurs have made frequent appearances in comic books and graphic novels, often as characters in fantastical stories or as the subjects of educational comics. Titles like "Cadillacs and Dinosaurs" blend science fiction with prehistoric themes, while others, like "Age of Reptiles" by Ricardo Delgado, offer wordless stories that depict the lives of dinosaurs in stunning detail. These visual narratives allow artists to explore the prehistoric world in creative and imaginative ways.

Fact 250: Dinosaurs Represent a Link Between Science and Imagination

Ultimately, dinosaurs represent a unique intersection of science and imagination. They are real creatures that once walked the Earth, yet their lives and behaviors remain shrouded in mystery. This blend of fact and fiction allows dinosaurs to occupy a special place in popular culture, where they can be both subjects of serious scientific study and icons of fantastical storytelling. Whether in a museum, a movie, or a child's imagination, dinosaurs continue to captivate us, bridging the gap between the ancient past and the present.

Chapter 9: Dinosaurs and the Future

What's Next for Our Understanding of Dinosaurs?

The study of dinosaurs is far from over. In fact, with each new discovery and technological advancement, our understanding of these ancient creatures continues to grow. As we look to the future, there are exciting possibilities on the horizon—new fossil discoveries, cutting-edge research, and even the potential to bring dinosaurs back to life, at least in some form. In this chapter, we'll explore what the future holds for the study of dinosaurs and how these ancient creatures might continue to influence our world.

Fact 251: New Fossil Discoveries Are Constantly Being Made

The fossil record is far from complete, and new dinosaur fossils are being discovered every year. These finds continue to expand our knowledge of dinosaur diversity, behavior, and evolution. With many remote and unexplored regions still out there, paleontologists believe that some of the most exciting discoveries may still be ahead of us. Each new fossil has the potential to rewrite what we know about the prehistoric world.

Fact 252: Advances in Technology Are Revolutionizing Paleontology

Technological advances are transforming the field of paleontology. Techniques like 3D scanning, CT imaging, and laser-stimulated fluorescence are allowing scientists to study fossils in unprecedented detail. These technologies are helping paleontologists uncover new information about dinosaur anatomy, behavior, and even color. As these tools become more sophisticated, our ability to analyze and interpret fossils will continue to improve.

Fact 253: DNA and Molecular Research Could Unlock New Insights

While extracting intact dinosaur DNA remains a significant challenge, advancements in molecular biology are opening new avenues for research. Scientists are studying proteins, collagen, and other organic molecules preserved in fossils to learn more about dinosaur biology. These studies could provide insights into dinosaur genetics, evolution, and how they relate to modern animals, particularly birds.

Fact 254: The Search for Dinosaur Soft Tissues Continues

The discovery of soft tissues in some dinosaur fossils has generated excitement and controversy in the scientific community. If more examples of preserved soft tissues are found, they could offer invaluable information about dinosaur physiology and behavior. Researchers are developing new methods to search for and analyze these tissues, which could lead to groundbreaking discoveries in paleontology.

Fact 255: The Potential for Dinosaur Cloning is Debated

The idea of cloning dinosaurs, popularized by the "Jurassic Park" franchise, remains a topic of speculation and debate. While the recreation of dinosaurs from ancient DNA is currently beyond our technological capabilities, advances in genetic engineering and de-extinction science are raising questions about what might be possible in the future. Scientists are exploring the ethical and technical challenges of bringing extinct species back to life, though dinosaurs remain a distant and unlikely possibility.

Fact 256: Dinosaur-Themed Augmented Reality (AR) and Virtual Reality (VR) Experiences Are Growing

As AR and VR technologies become more advanced, they are providing new ways to experience dinosaurs. From educational apps that bring dinosaurs to life in your living room to immersive VR simulations that allow you to explore prehistoric worlds, these technologies are making it easier than ever to learn about dinosaurs in engaging and interactive ways. These experiences are likely to become even more realistic and accessible in the future.

Fact 257: Citizen Science is Playing a Role in Dinosaur Discoveries

Citizen science, where members of the public participate in scientific research, is increasingly contributing to paleontology. Amateur fossil hunters, students, and enthusiasts are making significant discoveries and helping to analyze data. Projects like online databases and crowdsourced fossil identification are allowing more people to get involved in the search for dinosaurs, democratizing the field of paleontology.

Fact 258: The Study of Ancient Ecosystems is Providing Context for Dinosaur Research

Understanding the ecosystems in which dinosaurs lived is crucial for interpreting their behavior and evolution. By studying ancient climates, plant life, and other organisms that lived alongside dinosaurs, scientists are building a more comprehensive picture of the prehistoric world. This research helps to contextualize dinosaur fossils and provides insights into how these animals interacted with their environment.

Fact 259: The Future of Paleontology May Include Space Exploration

Some scientists are looking beyond Earth for clues about life in the universe, and the study of ancient life forms like dinosaurs could play a role in space exploration. By understanding how life on Earth evolved and adapted to changing conditions, researchers hope to better understand the potential for life on other planets. The techniques developed for studying fossils could one day be applied to analyzing extraterrestrial life forms or fossils found on other planets.

Fact 260: Dinosaurs Will Continue to Inspire Science Fiction and Art

Dinosaurs have long been a source of inspiration for science fiction and art, and this trend shows no signs of slowing down. As new discoveries are made, they will likely inspire new stories, films, and artistic interpretations. Dinosaurs will continue to captivate the human imagination, serving as symbols of both the wonders of the natural world and the mysteries that still await discovery.

Fact 261: Global Collaborations Are Advancing Dinosaur Research

Paleontology is increasingly becoming a global field, with scientists from around the world collaborating on research projects and fossil excavations. These collaborations are leading to more comprehensive studies and a greater sharing of knowledge and resources. As international cooperation in science grows, so too will our understanding of dinosaurs and the ancient world.

Fact 262: Dinosaurs in Education Will Evolve with New Technologies

As technology continues to evolve, so will the ways in which dinosaurs are taught in schools and universities. Interactive models, virtual field trips, and online learning platforms are already transforming how students engage with paleontology. Future generations of students will likely have access to even more advanced tools, allowing them to explore the world of dinosaurs in ways that were previously unimaginable.

Fact 263: The Ethics of De-Extinction Are Being Debated

The possibility of bringing extinct species back to life raises important ethical questions. While de-extinction could potentially help restore lost ecosystems, it also presents challenges related to biodiversity, conservation, and the impact on existing species. As science advances, these ethical considerations will become increasingly important, particularly if the idea of resurrecting dinosaurs ever moves from fiction to reality.

Fact 264: Advances in Fossil Imaging Are Uncovering New Species

New imaging technologies, such as synchrotron radiation and advanced CT scanning, are allowing scientists to study fossils in greater detail than ever before. These techniques are revealing new species that were previously hidden within rock or overlooked due to their small size or delicate structure. As these technologies improve, the discovery of new dinosaur species is likely to accelerate.

Fact 265: The Legacy of Dinosaurs Will Continue to Influence Science and Culture

Dinosaurs have left an indelible mark on both science and popular culture, and their legacy will continue to influence future generations. Whether through new scientific discoveries, advancements in technology, or their continued presence in art and media, dinosaurs will remain a powerful symbol of the natural world and the ongoing quest to understand our planet's history.

Fact 266: New Fossil Sites Are Still Being Discovered

Despite centuries of exploration, new fossil sites continue to be discovered around the world. These sites have the potential to yield important new species and provide insights into previously unexplored periods of dinosaur evolution. Paleontologists are particularly interested in regions that have been less studied, such as parts of Africa, Asia, and South America, where the fossil record may hold many more surprises.

Fact 267: Advances in Climate Science Are Helping to Reconstruct Dinosaur Habitats

Climate science is playing an increasingly important role in reconstructing the habitats of dinosaurs. By studying ancient climate data, such as ice cores and sediment layers, scientists are able to model the environments in which dinosaurs lived. This research is helping to explain how dinosaurs adapted to different climates and how environmental changes may have influenced their evolution and extinction.

Fact 268: The Future of Dinosaur Research May Include Space-Based Observations

As space technology advances, there may be opportunities to study Earth's history from space. Satellites and other space-based observatories could be used to detect fossil-rich areas, study geological formations, and even identify potential impact sites from space. This approach could open up new avenues for paleontological research and provide a broader perspective on Earth's ancient history.

Fact 269: Genetic Research Could Uncover More Dinosaur Relatives

Genetic research is revealing new connections between dinosaurs and other species, particularly birds. As our understanding of genetics deepens, scientists may uncover more distant relatives of dinosaurs and learn more about the evolutionary paths that led to modern species. This research could provide a more complete picture of the dinosaur family tree and their place in the broader context of life on Earth.

Fact 270: Dinosaurs Will Continue to Be a Source of Wonder and Discovery

The study of dinosaurs has always been driven by a sense of wonder and the desire to uncover the mysteries of the past. As new discoveries are made and new technologies are developed, this sense of wonder will continue to drive the field forward. Dinosaurs will remain a powerful reminder of Earth's rich and varied history, inspiring future generations to explore, discover, and learn.

Chapter 10: Dinosaurs and the Environment

How Dinosaurs Shaped and Were Shaped by Their World

Dinosaurs lived in a world that was very different from today's Earth. Over their 165-million-year reign, they adapted to changing climates, shifting continents, and evolving ecosystems. In turn, they played a significant role in shaping the environments they inhabited. In this chapter, we'll explore how dinosaurs interacted with their environment, how they adapted to changes, and how they influenced the world around them.

Fact 271: Dinosaurs Lived in Diverse Habitats

Dinosaurs thrived in a wide range of environments, from lush tropical forests to arid deserts and polar regions. The fossil record shows that dinosaurs were incredibly adaptable, with species living on every continent, including Antarctica. This diversity in habitats reflects the dinosaurs' ability to evolve and thrive in different climates and conditions, making them one of the most successful groups of animals in Earth's history.

Fact 272: Continental Drift Shaped Dinosaur Evolution

During the Mesozoic Era, the continents were not arranged as they are today. Instead, they were joined together in a supercontinent called Pangaea, which began to break apart around 200 million years ago. This process of continental drift had a profound impact on dinosaur evolution, as it created new landmasses, isolated populations, and led to the development of distinct dinosaur faunas on different continents. As the continents drifted apart, dinosaurs adapted to the changing environments and the challenges they presented.

Fact 273: Dinosaurs Played a Role in Shaping Vegetation

Dinosaurs, particularly the large herbivores, played a significant role in shaping the vegetation of their time. By feeding on vast amounts of plant material, dinosaurs influenced the distribution and abundance of different plant species. Some plants evolved defenses like thorns or toxic compounds to deter herbivorous dinosaurs, while others thrived in the disturbed environments created by grazing. This dynamic relationship between dinosaurs and plants helped shape the ecosystems of the Mesozoic Era.

Fact 274: Climate Change Was a Constant Challenge for Dinosaurs

Throughout the Mesozoic Era, the Earth's climate underwent significant changes. Periods of global warming and cooling, fluctuations in sea levels, and changes in atmospheric composition all presented challenges for dinosaurs. Some species adapted to these changes by evolving new physical traits or migrating to more favorable environments. However, the ability of dinosaurs to cope with climate change varied, and some groups declined or went extinct as a result of these environmental shifts.

Fact 275: Dinosaurs and the Carbon Cycle

Dinosaurs played a role in the Earth's carbon cycle by contributing to the breakdown of organic matter and the cycling of nutrients. Large herbivorous dinosaurs, such as sauropods, consumed vast amounts of plant material, and their waste products helped fertilize the soil and promote plant growth. This process was an important part of the carbon cycle, which regulates the Earth's climate by controlling the levels of carbon dioxide in the atmosphere.

Fact 276: Dinosaurs Lived Through the Mesozoic Greenhouse Climate

The Mesozoic Era is often referred to as a "greenhouse world" due to the warm, humid climate that prevailed for much of this period. High levels of carbon dioxide in the atmosphere led to elevated global temperatures, with little to no polar ice caps. This warm climate allowed tropical and subtropical ecosystems to extend further towards the poles, creating a world where dinosaurs could thrive in a wide variety of environments.

Fact 277: Dinosaur Migration Patterns Were Influenced by Seasonal Changes

Many dinosaurs, particularly the large herbivores, likely migrated in response to seasonal changes in their environment. Fossilized trackways and isotopic analysis of bones suggest that some species traveled long distances to find food and water as the seasons changed. These migrations would have been crucial for survival, particularly in regions with extreme seasonal variations, such as high-latitude areas where daylight and food availability fluctuated dramatically throughout the year.

Fact 278: The Rise of Flowering Plants Changed Dinosaur Diets

Flowering plants, or angiosperms, began to diversify during the Cretaceous period, leading to significant changes in dinosaur diets. As these plants became more common, herbivorous dinosaurs adapted to new food sources. Some dinosaurs developed specialized teeth and jaws for processing the tougher, fibrous material of flowering plants. The spread of angiosperms also led to new ecological relationships, as dinosaurs became important pollinators and seed dispersers for these plants.

Fact 279: Dinosaurs and the Water Cycle

Dinosaurs were an integral part of the water cycle in their ecosystems. Large herbivores, in particular, needed substantial amounts of water to survive and likely played a role in shaping the distribution of water sources such as rivers, lakes, and wetlands. By altering vegetation patterns and the landscape through their feeding and movement, dinosaurs influenced the hydrology of their environments, contributing to the overall functioning of the water cycle.

Fact 280: The Impact of Dinosaurs on Soil Formation

Dinosaurs contributed to soil formation through their activities, such as trampling vegetation, digging, and the decomposition of their bodies. These processes helped break down organic matter, mix soil layers, and introduce nutrients that promoted plant growth. The presence of large herbivores would have created disturbances in the soil, encouraging the development of diverse plant communities and contributing to the health and fertility of Mesozoic ecosystems.

Fact 281: Dinosaurs and the Nitrogen Cycle

The nitrogen cycle, which is essential for the growth of plants and the health of ecosystems, was influenced by dinosaurs through their feeding and waste products. Herbivorous dinosaurs consumed nitrogen-rich plants and excreted waste that returned nitrogen to the soil, making it available for other plants to use. This recycling of nutrients was a critical part of maintaining the balance of ecosystems and supporting the diverse plant and animal life of the Mesozoic Era.

Fact 282: Dinosaurs Lived Through Periods of Volcanic Activity

Volcanic activity was a common feature of the Mesozoic landscape, and dinosaurs lived through numerous volcanic eruptions. These eruptions could have both immediate and long-term effects on the environment, including the release of ash and gases, changes in climate, and the creation of new habitats. Some volcanic events, like those that formed the Deccan Traps, may have contributed to the extinction of certain dinosaur species by altering the climate and ecosystems in which they lived.

Fact 283: Dinosaurs and the Oxygen Levels of the Mesozoic Era

Oxygen levels in the atmosphere varied throughout the Mesozoic Era, influencing the physiology and behavior of dinosaurs. During periods of higher oxygen levels, dinosaurs may have been able to grow larger and sustain higher levels of activity. Conversely, lower oxygen levels could have limited the size and metabolic rates of some species. The relationship between dinosaurs and atmospheric oxygen is an ongoing area of research, with implications for understanding how these animals adapted to their environment.

Fact 284: Dinosaur Interactions with Other Species

Dinosaurs did not exist in isolation—they interacted with a variety of other species, including plants, insects, mammals, and marine life. These interactions played a crucial role in shaping the ecosystems of the Mesozoic Era. For example, predation by dinosaurs influenced the evolution of prey species, while the presence of large herbivores affected the distribution and composition of plant communities. These complex interactions helped maintain the balance of ecosystems and contributed to the overall diversity of life during this time.

Fact 285: Dinosaurs and the Evolution of Modern Ecosystems

The ecosystems that existed during the age of dinosaurs laid the groundwork for the modern ecosystems we see today. Many of the plants and animals that lived alongside dinosaurs, such as ferns, conifers, and early mammals, are ancestors of modern species. The interactions between dinosaurs and their environment helped shape the evolutionary paths of these species, influencing the development of the ecosystems that would emerge after the dinosaurs went extinct.

Fact 286: The Influence of Dinosaurs on Earth's Geology

Dinosaurs, particularly the large sauropods, could have had a significant impact on Earth's geology. Their massive size and weight would have contributed to soil compaction, erosion, and the formation of sedimentary layers. The footprints and trackways left by dinosaurs have been preserved in rock formations around the world, providing a record of their movement and behavior that has endured for millions of years.

Fact 287: Dinosaurs Adapted to a Changing World

Dinosaurs were highly adaptable creatures, capable of evolving in response to the changing environments of the Mesozoic Era. As continents drifted, climates shifted, and new plant and animal species emerged, dinosaurs evolved new traits and behaviors to survive. This adaptability was key to their success and longevity, allowing them to thrive in a wide range of environments for over 160 million years.

Fact 288: The Role of Dinosaurs in Nutrient Cycling

Dinosaurs played a crucial role in nutrient cycling within their ecosystems. By consuming plants and animals, and through their waste products, dinosaurs helped recycle nutrients back into the soil, promoting plant growth and supporting the overall health of their environment. This cycling of nutrients was essential for maintaining the productivity and stability of Mesozoic ecosystems.

Fact 289: The Legacy of Dinosaurs in Modern Ecosystems

Although dinosaurs went extinct 66 million years ago, their legacy continues in modern ecosystems. The evolutionary innovations that arose during the age of dinosaurs, such as flowering plants, birds, and certain types of insects, have shaped the biodiversity we see today. Additionally, the fossils and trackways left behind by dinosaurs provide valuable information about past environments, helping scientists understand how ecosystems have changed over time.

Fact 290: Dinosaurs and the Earth's Biological History

Dinosaurs are a key part of Earth's biological history, representing one of the most successful and diverse groups of animals to ever exist. Their interactions with the environment, their adaptations to changing conditions, and their role in shaping ecosystems have left an indelible mark on the planet. Studying dinosaurs and their environment not only helps us understand the past but also provides insights into the processes that continue to shape life on Earth today.

Conclusion: The Enduring Legacy of Dinosaurs

A Journey Through Time and Science

Dinosaurs, despite having been extinct for millions of years, continue to captivate the imagination of people around the world. Their size, diversity, and the mystery surrounding their sudden disappearance have made them a subject of endless fascination and study. Throughout this book, we've explored the many facets of dinosaur life, from their evolution and behavior to their role in popular culture and modern science. As we conclude our journey through the world of dinosaurs, it's clear that these ancient creatures have left an indelible mark on both our planet and our understanding of life itself.

The study of dinosaurs is far from complete. With each new fossil discovery and technological advancement, we peel back another layer of the prehistoric world, uncovering new insights and raising new questions. Dinosaurs are not just a window into the past; they are also a mirror reflecting our curiosity, our quest for knowledge, and our deep connection to the natural world.

Fact 291: Dinosaurs Are a Symbol of Evolutionary Success

Dinosaurs were incredibly successful, dominating Earth for over 160 million years. This longevity is a testament to their adaptability and resilience, allowing them to survive and thrive in a wide range of environments and climates. Their success serves as a powerful reminder of the ever-changing nature of life on Earth and the importance of adaptability in the face of environmental challenges.

Fact 292: Birds Are Living Dinosaurs

One of the most significant scientific discoveries of the last century is the realization that birds are the direct descendants of theropod dinosaurs. This means that, in a sense, dinosaurs are not entirely extinct—every bird we see today is a living representative of the dinosaur lineage. This connection has reshaped our understanding of both dinosaurs and birds, highlighting the continuity of life through evolution.

Fact 293: Dinosaurs Inspire Ongoing Scientific Discovery

The study of dinosaurs continues to inspire new scientific discoveries, not just in paleontology but also in related fields like genetics, geology, and climate science. Dinosaurs provide a unique opportunity to study the processes of evolution, extinction, and adaptation, offering lessons that are relevant to understanding the history of life on Earth and the challenges that lie ahead.

Fact 294: Dinosaurs Are a Gateway to Understanding Earth's History

Dinosaurs are more than just fascinating creatures—they are key to understanding the history of our planet. The study of dinosaurs involves exploring the geological record, deciphering ancient climates, and understanding the movements of continents over millions of years. In this way, dinosaurs serve as a gateway to understanding the complex and dynamic history of Earth itself.

Fact 295: Dinosaur Fossils Are Found in Unexpected Places

Dinosaur fossils have been discovered in some of the most unexpected places, from the cold deserts of Antarctica to the bustling streets of major cities. These finds remind us that the Earth's surface has changed dramatically over time and that the remains of these ancient creatures can be found in the most surprising locations.

Fact 296: The Study of Dinosaurs Is Global

Paleontology is a global science, with dinosaur fossils being studied by scientists all over the world. International collaborations and fossil discoveries in places like China, Argentina, and Africa are helping to build a more complete picture of dinosaur diversity and evolution, showing that these creatures were truly global in their distribution.

Fact 297: Dinosaurs Continue to Educate and Entertain

Dinosaurs have become a staple of education and entertainment, captivating audiences of all ages. From museums and documentaries to movies and books, dinosaurs are used to teach important scientific concepts and to inspire wonder about the natural world. Their ability to engage and educate is unmatched, making them a powerful tool for science communication.

Fact 298: Dinosaurs Are Used in Modern Environmental Education

The story of the dinosaurs, particularly their extinction, is often used to teach about modern environmental issues, such as climate change and biodiversity loss. By understanding the factors that led to the dinosaurs' demise, we can draw parallels to current environmental challenges and the importance of protecting Earth's ecosystems.

Fact 299: Dinosaurs Represent the Intersection of Science and Imagination

Dinosaurs occupy a unique space at the intersection of science and imagination. While they are the subject of serious scientific study, they also inspire creativity in art, literature, and film. This dual role makes dinosaurs a powerful symbol of human curiosity and the endless possibilities of exploration and discovery.

Fact 300: The Legacy of Dinosaurs Will Continue to Grow

As long as there are questions to be answered and mysteries to be solved, the legacy of dinosaurs will continue to grow. Future generations of scientists, students, and enthusiasts will build on the work of those who came before, deepening our understanding of these ancient creatures and their place in the history of life on Earth.

A Final Thought

Dinosaurs, in all their diversity and grandeur, remind us of the incredible history of life on our planet. They represent both the fragility and the resilience of life, the ongoing process of evolution, and the endless curiosity that drives scientific inquiry. As we continue to explore and learn from these ancient creatures, we also gain a deeper appreciation for the world we live in today and the forces that have shaped it.

Made in the USA
Columbia, SC
21 October 2024

44833890R00059